Finding Constance, Searching for Adventure, Finding Faith, and Everything in Between

Connie Leahr

© 2021 by Connie Leahr. All rights reserved.

Words Matter Publishing
P.O. Box 531
Salem, Il 62881
www.wordsmatterpublishing.com

No part of this publication may be reproduced, stored in a retrieval system, or transmitted in any way by any means—electronic, mechanical, photocopy, recording, or otherwise—without the prior permission of the copyright holder, except as provided by USA copyright law.

ISBN: 978-1-953912-24-4

Library of Congress Catalog Card Number: 2021943146

Preface

I am so thankful for my Christian heritage. It is such a blessing to have memories of grandparents and parents who loved the Lord and set an example for me to live by, even though I didn't always do it. Aunts and uncles as well. There have been a few in our family on both sides who have passed away that we don't know for sure they are with Jesus today, but only a few. How blessed we are.

I thank God for my wonderful family, especially my children who have blessed my life more than I could ever have hoped for. God has been so good to us. We have all had our ups and downs, but God loves us and has taken loving care of us. I am writing this story of my life in the hope that my children and grandchildren will profit by my many mistakes. I know that some already have, for they have told me so. I can tell others have because of the way they have managed their lives and listened for God's direction.

I hope you all enjoy my attempt to put this story into words in a way that will convey my feelings to you as well as relate stories I think valuable or entertaining. I certainly would hope no one feels offended or left out. And if all of my facts are not exact, well, you know me...as long as I get my point across, that is what matters!

Table of Contents

Chapter One: Before The Beginning 1
Chapter Two: Really Getting Started 11
Chapter Three: Better Times Coming 23
Chapter Four: Growing Up 37
Chapter Five: High School 43
Chapter Six: Real Life 55
Chapter Seven: Marriage 61
Chapter Eight: Babies, Bottles And Broken Dreams 71
Chapter Nine: Giving Up 81
Chapter Ten: Trying Not To Give Up 89
Chapter Eleven: Moving To The Big House 101
Chapter Twelve: The Big Adventure 109
Chapter Thirteen: The Wasted Years 115
Chapter Fourteen: Roller Coaster Ride 123
Chapter Fifteen: Pain And Gain 133
Chapter Sixteen: The Winter Of My Content 145
Chapter Seventeen: One More Time 157
Chapter Eighteen: Grown Children 167
Chapter Nineteen: In The End 181
Chapter Twenty: My Testimony For Jesus 187
From the Kids... 195

My Story

Chapter One

Before The Beginning

On a warm spring evening in 1932 a group of teenagers met in a small community in Illinois by the name of Milton. The supposed purpose of this meeting was to play hide and seek. Of course it was just a coincidence that there were three boys and three girls who all knew each other. Two boys and one girl were from the Ernest Moore family.

Their names were Leland, Helen, and Kelly. Two girls were from the Lucian and Cora Smith family. Their names were Fay and Martha. The other boy in the group was named Arlo Dulaney. It was rumored among the younger set in that small community that Arlo was Helen Moore's beau, but as the story goes, Helen didn't see it that way.

Nevertheless, she was willing to participate in the fun much to everyone else's delight. All three of the girls were friends but the Smith girls had more in mind than spending time with Helen. Martha had set her sights on developing a 'special relationship' with Leland Moore. Some thought that Fay may have had the same thing in mind, but Martha saw to it that nothing developed for Fay. It seems Martha was a more determined young lady than her sister. Either that or perhaps Fay wasn't interested. Or could it be that Leland had the same thought as Martha? Whatever the plans may have been, it turned out that Martha had her way. They became a couple soon after that summer evening of fun and the only time Martha had any doubt as to who had won Leland's heart was when he took her for a bike ride one evening and then he took Fay for a longer bike ride. When they returned to their starting point, Martha let her feelings be made known to both of them. As far as anyone knows there was never another time that Leland paid any attention to another girl, especially Fay!

One day Martha was walking home from the store carrying groceries for her mother. She went out of her way to walk past the Moore residence, even though her burden included a five pound bag of sugar. To her great satisfaction, Leland just happened to be outside and saw her. He quickly stopped what he was doing and rushed to her aid, offering to carry the groceries to the house for her. That was the beginning of their permanent relationship and sets the stage for the story of my life. Martha was fourteen years old and Leland was nineteen. They dated for two and a half years. During that time the Smith family moved a few miles away to a tiny village named Time. The Smith family had moved to Milton from Time because their house burned and there was no house available in Time for them to rent. Mr. Smith had to walk the four miles to and from his blacksmith shop in Time every day as long as they lived in Milton. It was about a year before an old house was offered to the Smith family south of Time. It was going to be rent free for it had been empty for years. Leland helped Mr. Smith do what had to be done to the house so his family could survive there. There were no window lights or steps up to the porch. It was a very poor place to live but better than walking eight miles a day to and from work.

This made the courtship of Martha and Leland more difficult because there were times Leland could not get to Time. He sometimes didn't have a dime to buy a gallon of gas. By this time he had a Ford Model T. They pursued the relationship anyway. Leland even went to pick Martha and Fay up (when he had the money for gas) and took them to and from school (they were both freshman in high school at Milton). Leland had quit school at the end of his sophomore year. He just wasn't interested in school, but the girls were. They loved it and it broke Martha's heart when she had to quit at the end of the year simply because there was no money for books or clothing. Eventually Martha got a job in Pittsfield working for a family who had a new baby and needed someone to do the housework, cooking, and laundry for the family until the mother was able to do it herself. Things were done a lot differently back then and childbirth was thought to be reason for a woman to stay in bed for two weeks and then do very little for weeks after that. This job security gave Martha and Leland enough confidence to decide marriage was their answer to the hardship of not being together enough. On November 5th, 1934 they sneaked away with another couple and both couples were married by a Justice of the Peace in Winchester, IL. Martha was sixteen and Leland was twenty-one. They kept the marriage a secret for a while because they could not afford a place to live. However, they couldn't stand that situation so they got up the nerve to make their announcement. I never heard much about their parents' reactions except to say that Mr. Smith was happy for them, but Mr. Moore was not. They lived with the Smith family for about a month, but they were too poor to support them. Then they lived with Leland's folks for about six weeks. That was an unbearable situation on everyone's part and when a man named Pat Wallace and his wife Phoebe offered to let them live in two rooms in the back of their house, they gratefully accepted. This was soon to become an undesirable situation as well. A house that was little more than a shack was purchased by contract for deed by Leland's father and he allowed the young couple to clean it up and live there if they would pay the mortgage payments of $10.00 a month. To them it was home and they began their life together in earnest. This young couple would one day be my parents.

The Great Depression was slowly coming to an end in the early years of my parents' marriage and by 1937 it was pretty much over, though things were still terribly difficult. Franklin D. Roosevelt was president of the United States and he implemented the first and only dignified method of welfare. He signed into law a new program for unemployed people called WPA meaning "Workmen Participation Assistance". (Most people jokingly called it "We Piddle Around"). My father was quick to sign up for this program and as a result, helped build our local swimming pool and shelter house at King Park in Pittsfield, IL. He did this long before our family moved to Pittsfield and that opportunity greatly improved their lives. So much so that this was when my mother decided she could wait no longer to have her first baby. Dad did not agree! Being the oldest of six living children in his family he had had enough of taking care of kids. However, my mother's desire was so great that she cried, begged, and even threatened to leave if he wouldn't give in. And so, after nearly three years of marriage, when Mom was nineteen years old and Dad was twenty-four, they became the parents of a baby girl.

I was named Constance Ann and my mother could not have been happier. Dad had to put in so many long hours working and traveling back and forth that I can't think there was much time for me to make him sorry he was a Dad.

I have a few delightful memories of my early childhood that I love to tell. Probably because they were fondly told to others often as I was growing up. There were bad things too, of course, but I don't remember much about the bad. That in itself is a gift from God.

The bad thing that happened that has been talked about through the years is the fact that when I was about a year old I became very ill. The disease was finally diagnosed as Acrodynia (nick named pink disease because of prolonged fever--hence flushed complexion). It was an extended illness of about a year and it eventually became necessary for me to be taken to St. Louis' Children's Hospital for treatment. The cause of the disease was thought to be mercury poisoning. I don't know if that was ever proven. The disease was very rare and not much research was ever done. Mom and Dad had very little money. While Dad worked every day, Mom did hair for several ladies in town (who could afford it) for 10 cents a head. That was long before you had to go to school and get a license to wash and pin up someone's hair! The government was too busy trying to take care of poor people to think up ways to tax them to death. That came later!

One day I remember Mom working on a lady's hair in the kitchen while the lady's son, who was older than I was, was pushing me in my little swing that Dad had rigged up for me on the back porch. The boy's mother cautioned him not to push me too high. As the ride was beginning to get a little too exciting for me, I wondered how she knew he was pushing me too high. I didn't know that moms just know! Looking back at that as I write this story, I have to wonder how much of a sacrifice it was for Dad to come up with the rope and a board to make that swing.

Another day I remember Mom was washing my hair and when she got it good and soapy, she sculpted it up into a long point right on top of my head. Then she lifted me up so I could see what I looked like in the mirror. I immediately became hysterical. I remember her soft laughter as she comforted me and assured me it would be OK. After my curly hair was dry and my bath was over, Mom dressed me up and took me outside to take my picture with her Brownie Box camera. There was a large gunny sack full of walnuts in the yard and she told me to sit there and smile for her. As I primly sat down and began pulling my dress down before smiling, I heard the camera click. I became angry with her because I knew she had done that on purpose thinking it was cute and I was not ready yet! I was very unhappy at the idea of a picture without a smile. That picture has always been a favorite in the family album.

My favorite early childhood memory would have to be the Christmas after my third birthday. Having no fear of the dark, I got up in the wee hours of the morning to see if Santa had been there yet. I don't remember if l woke Mom and Dad on purpose, but they were up. It could very well be that they had not even gotten to bed. There was this beautiful dark red table and two little chairs there under the tree.

The table had a little tablecloth on it and was set with beautiful little tin dishes. In one of the chairs was a pretty little doll and the other was awaiting the pleasure of my presence. I was overwhelmed at Santa' s generosity in giving me the doll and the dishes, but I knew my daddy had made that table and chairs! I said "Oh, Daddy, you didn't have to do that". They looked at each other with pleasure and surprise and I knew

I was correct in my assumption. There were very few other Christmas mornings in my childhood significant enough for me to remember specific details. The ones that were significant involved my dad in some special way. In writing this particular memory, I think I just learned a little more how important a child's father is. If I would allow it, this could give me more reason for regrets in my later life. Sadly, nothing can be changed by regrets realized too late.

Getting back to my illness, needless to say my parents had little money, and no car. Not to mention the fact that Dad's driving experience included only a small portion of Pike county. It was financially and even physically impossible for them to take me to St. Louis. A neighbor man named Merle Hoover, who was old enough to be my grandfather and had been blessed with plenty, offered his assistance. He not only drove our family to St. Louis to see the doctors there but paid the expenses of the trip and the medical bills! I cannot remember that man because he died while I was still very young. I remember his wife and daughter, though, and I always loved them but I didn't know why. It probably has to do with the fact that they loved me and paid lots of attention to me. I am told that everyone in the neighborhood paid attention to me. Particularly since I had been so very ill for so long. It was about a year before I could be considered completely recovered.

And then, when I was just past three years old, Mom became pregnant again. She was terribly sick with morning sickness and I was a handful, so "Granny Bide" helped a lot with me. She was my Dad's mother and her name was Vida. I couldn't pronounce it correctly, so she became "Granny Bide". I always loved her dearly. She was plump and jolly and always made you feel so special. Grandmas have a way of doing that.

My other grandmother was always "Grammy" and I loved her dearly too. She was quieter than Granny Bide but loving and funny and as sweet as she could be. I was blessed with wonderful Christian grandparents as well as Christian parents and most aunts and uncles. The women in the family always had much more influence on me than the men, spiritually speaking. My younger sister was closer to Grammy than I was simply because we did not have the opportunity to visit her often until she moved to Pittsfield just two houses from us. By that time I was getting up in grade school and much too busy with my own life to pay much attention to her. Karen, being four years younger, knew a good thing when she saw it. Grammy always called her "my little doll babe" and spoiled her rotten, giving her some things (such as coffee) that she was not allowed at home. One time she told Karen a story of her childhood that was most interesting. Her family had moved from Illinois to Oklahoma in a covered wagon when she was nine years old. There were many hardships including the possibility of Indian attack.

However, being a kid, Grammy chose to enjoy the lighter side. It seems there was an uncle who was not very well liked by the children in the family, so they played at least one trick on him that she told Karen about. They had to tie things in the wagons securely so they would not fall out when they were crossing creeks or ravines that had embankments on either side. One day some of the kids, including Gram, decided to untie the things in "Uncle's" wagon. When they crossed the next creek, all of his pots and pans and who knows what else, fell out into the water. I don't know if he ever figured out who did it, but I feel sorry for them if he did! There were probably many more stories, but Karen says she was never able to get her to talk about it again.

Martha & Fay

Leland & Bessie

Leland

Leland and Martha before they married

Chapter Two
Really Getting Started

The next early memory is one of our family coming into Pittsfield in a car. I am not sure when Dad was able to buy a car, but it was our car, and I was sitting on Mom's lap in the front seat. Her tummy was huge and I knew there was a baby in there. We were moving to Pittsfield so Dad could work for R.C. Gray as a mechanic in the Chevrolet garage. We moved into a three-room apartment on East Washington Street. The other part of the house was occupied by a family named Dorsey. They had two children, a daughter named Connie and a son. I do not remember the son or the father but I remember Connie and her mother. Connie and her brother were several years older than me and I felt very privileged that she sometimes invited me to sit in the porch swing with her or to join in the fun when she had a girlfriend over. I think she felt pleased that we shared the same name. She was also at the age when girls really enjoy little kids. She was probably 10 or 12 years old.

I remember nothing of the actual moving in and making a home out of the apartment. I just remember the car ride, sitting on Mom's lap, noticing her fat tummy and knowing that there was a baby in there. What an adventure for Mom and Dad and yet to me it was just another day in the life of a child. It was the beginning of several adventures that I remember during the couple of years we lived in that apartment. I am sure it was a happy time for my parents. This was the first real job away from farm jobs that were not very secure that Dad had after the great depression was over. He no longer had to depend on F.D.R.'s workman's compensation program, though Dad was forever grateful for that Federal Program that was a life saver to so very many families.

I can, to this day, remember the arrangement of that apartment. It seemed like a fine home to me, but I soon realized that there were things that my parents didn't like about it after being there just a short while. Specifically, the neighbor lady! I never knew why but I didn't like her either, simply because of bits and pieces of conversation I heard about her. I was to learn many years later that most of it was because she was very nosey and rather bossy (as if the place belonged to her)! It turned out that she was extremely helpful in times of need but I am not sure it was enough "goodness" to neutralize the bad effects of her personality on Mom and Dad. They felt that even in her helpfulness there was an element of "nosey".

Two days after my fourth birthday, I found myself in the care of Mrs. Dorsey in her apartment, much to my dismay! I was aware that Mom was having her baby and I definitely thought that I should be allowed to be there and know what was going on. Mrs. Dorsey, however, was more than determined that it wasn't going to happen. At one point she informed me that she had to make a trip to the toilet and she wanted me to go with her. I could envision the opportunity to get into my own house while she was in the toilet, so I tried to talk her out of making me go in with her. It was no use. She wasn't about to take any chances!

The next thing I knew I was inside that smelly little building with her. As she turned around to sit down I backed up against the outside wall as far away from her as I could get. All of a sudden, there was a loud cracking noise and I realized the floor had caved in! I was standing on a ledge about a foot wide just to the left of the door and Mrs. Dorsey was screaming at the top of her lungs, "go get your daddy, go get your daddy"!

I did so immediately! He was standing in the back yard just yards away from us and was talking to a friend of his when I came running out of the toilet screaming "Mrs. Dorsey fell in the toilet!" The friend's name was MacLuggage so naturally he was called "Mac." He said "I wonder how they will be able to tell which pile is Mrs. Dorsey!" I don't remember that because I was so young but Mom told me about it fifty five years later when I was visiting her in the nursing home. We had a big laugh over it. I don't have a clue what they did with me but I was not allowed to witness the rescue just as I was not allowed to watch Mom have a baby! There was so much going on and I missed it all.

Probably if I had paid more attention and been less frustrated, I could have at least heard something if I wasn't going to get to see anything! I have wondered if my desire to see Mrs. Dorsey in such a compromising situation might have had something to do with my dislike for her. Can children four years old experience such feelings? Probably not. I think it was just curiosity. How often does anybody get an opportunity like that?!

One day, after Mom was back on her feet, she was in the wash-shed doing the laundry. She had given me the responsibility of coming to get her if baby sister, Karen, cried or even woke up. Well, she woke up and she cried and I knew she probably needed a dry diaper. Instead of doing as I was told, I decided to help. I got the baby out of her bed and laid her on Mom and Dad's bed. I proceeded to remove the wet diaper and was carefully pinning on the dry one when Mom stepped into the room. She shrieked out the words, "Connie Ann, what do you think you are doing?" Before she could get the words out she was at my side taking over. I was shocked because I didn't get the praise I thought I would for being such a helper. I would come to understand her reaction years later when I had kids of my own.

Another day, I remember Mom deciding that the baby needed an enema (they did things like that back then). I was extremely interested in this process. I remember I had on a white pinafore that I was quite proud of and I was right on the front row during the entire process. All of a sudden there was a squirt and I was wearing yellow stuff on my white pinafore! Being quite nasty, I was in a state of disbelief that this had happened to me. I remember Mom telling me that I got what I deserved for thinking I had to have my nose stuck into everything she did.

One evening, after supper, I remember feeling a little sick. The next thing I knew I was throwing up. We had had pumpkin pie for supper and I thought (for years) that it had made me sick. I should have been so fortunate, not to mention the rest of the family. It was soon discovered that I was in the early stages of a second time around with Acrodynia. Again I was sick with high fever, hurting eyes, irritability, itching, no appetite, hair and teeth coming out, etc. I don't know how Mom survived it but she did because she had to. Karen was just a few months old, maybe close to a year. Just learning to walk and Mom said every time she got near me I would knock her down. I was like that with everyone. It was the beginning of a long hard journey for all of us.

It was not very long until the local doctors decided that I would again need medical treatment by the Doctors at St. Louis Children's Hospital. This time my dad's boss, Mr. R.C. Gray came to the rescue. He furnished a car and a friend of Dad's named Lyle Greenwood did the driving. I don't know who, if anyone, helped with expenses but the hospital and doctors in St. Louis did a lot of the work free of charge in the name of research. There were no records available to them of any child ever having this disease a second time. It was rare for anyone to have it at all.

The main doctor, an older man, whose name was John Zehorski was good to me and I really liked him. His son was also a doctor but I didn't like him. The senior doctor would give orders and the junior doctor would carry them out. It didn't take me long to figure out that the old doctor was nice to me and the young one did things that hurt! One day when junior doctor walked into the room, I announced to my mom, "I don't want anything from that damned doctor!" Which, of course, embarrassed her to death. He did what he came to do anyway. When the senior doctor told me I could go home at last, I asked him if I could keep the little nightgown I was wearing and he said "I think we can arrange that." It was white with pink trim. Somehow, I felt compensated for all they had put me through.

Being much older this time, there are several very unpleasant things I remember about the disease. Light hurt my eyes very badly and Mom had to keep the shades drawn or I could not stand the pain. One day she gave me some small squares of cloth and a needle and thread. She taught me how to sew quilt blocks together. I couldn't see because it was so dark in there and with tears running down my cheeks, I uttered several choice words and gave it up. I remember how frustrated and angry I was.

The most miserable symptom I had was a burning and itching of my hands and feet. Mom would sit on my bed as much as she could and scratch my hands and feet. I remember one day that Mrs. Dorsey sat on the bed too, scratching my feet while Mom did my hands. I was totally miserable, but I imagine I became totally spoiled too!

I remember my teeth coming out and because of conversations I heard I knew it was too soon because I was only four years old and the teeth still had big roots on them.

Mom saved some of the teeth and I have them in my baby book to this day. I didn't really mind giving up the teeth but maybe I used it for an excuse not to eat. I can remember Mom trying to coax me into eating and I had no interest in it. I was very cross and irritable and could have cared less if I hurt her feelings or worried her (or anyone else for that matter). Even my favorite cousin, Virginia, couldn't get near me.

Once again, I was sick for about a year. One day, in the later stages of my illness, while Mom was busy, I took advantage of an opportunity to put on my little bathrobe and sneak outside. I didn't feel like playing because I was just beginning to get better. I just wanted to sit in Mrs. Dorsey's porch swing and stare at the big outdoors. I think I was no longer running a fever but was still not allowed outside. I saw Mrs. Dorsey peeking around the comer at me and knew in an instant that my reprieve was over. Sure enough, in just a few moments,

Mom came around the corner saying, "what do you think you are doing, young lady?" I thought it was rather obvious what I thought I was doing but I soon found myself back in the house in spite of my objections and explanations! I was really mad at Mrs. Dorsey for a long time. Probably fifteen or twenty years!

After my recovery was complete, I made up for the deprivation I had suffered that day. I remember visiting the neighbors west of us one day. I thought they were strange because two men lived there and there was no "mom." However, it was a father and son who had lost their "mom." I remember nothing of the visit except the feeling of triumph I felt just because they let me in the house. They were nice to me, but it didn't take long for me to decide the thrill of getting in was all there was! I never had any desire to go back. I remember their name was Williams. To the east of us lived an elderly couple. I never got around to visiting them but I remember wanting to when I learned that the husband had died. In those days, the visitation was at the house and I was very curious about it. I couldn't imagine how it would feel to be in the house with a dead person. Something told me I had better not try to find out. I'm not sure if it was because I was afraid of the consequences of doing something wrong or if I was afraid of the dead person. At any rate, I am sure it was a good thing I didn't push my luck.

One day I decided to take a walk to a friend's house to see if she could play with me. Her mother told me she was taking a nap and did not invite me in. I decided to sit on the step and wait for her to wake up. How long could anyone sleep in the daytime? Well, the time went by slowly and I finally got tired of waiting. I started for home (about 2 blocks away) and when I came into view of the house I saw my dad standing in the yard. I knew he was supposed to be at work and I knew I was in trouble. You see, this was not the first time, maybe not even the fifteenth time, that I had gone off to play or explore without permission. In fact, I never asked permission because I knew the answer would be no. Well, I had been told several times by my dad that "one of these days I am going to tie you to a tree to teach you a lesson". I was shocked to find out this was the "time." After much scolding, Dad walked off toward his tool shed. When he came out he had a long piece of rope in his hand. He said, "come over here, I am going to tie you to that big tree over there." I thought he would surely not do such a thing. What would I do? What if someone saw me tied to that tree? Everyone would know I had been a bad girl! How can I keep anyone from seeing me? How long will he leave me there? I asked, "Daddy, how long are you going to leave me here?" as he was tying the rope around my waist. "All night long." came the answer. "Please, please, please, I will never do it again." No answer. He walked away and went into the house. When he came out he had an old blanket for me to sit on if I wanted to. He told me it was going to be my bed for the night. Then he went back to work. I don't remember seeing Mom at all but I'm sure she was watching out the window. (She told me years later that she was writing a letter to Merle Hoover when she realized what was going on). I laid down on the blanket so no one could see me and wondered what my fate would be.

Much later in the afternoon, I was happy to see my Dad coming home from work. It seemed like I had been tied up for hours and new hope swelled up in my heart as I saw him walking toward the house. He said "hi" to me and went on in the house. I thought he must have meant it when he said I had to stay there all night. If not, he surely would have untied me before he went inside. I began to sink into despair again, thinking

I was certainly doomed to a very long nocturnal nap. What was I going to do? About that time he came out the back door with a blanket draped over his arm! Despair! He really was going to leave me out there all night! He walked over near to where I sat and began spreading the blanket neatly on the grass. Then he walked away, back into the house. I was in a state of desperate disbelief. I sat there numbly wondering how I would survive this ordeal when he came back out the door with a bottle of orange soda in his hand. He came over to me and laid down on the blanket. Of course, I scrambled to his side and laid down beside him. At least he loved me enough to spend some time with me before carrying out my sentence! We shared the soda and talked, I'm sure about the hazards of a four-year-old wandering around the neighborhood all by herself, and that was the end of the story as I remember it. I did not have to stay out there tied to that tree all night, of course. When Mom called us in for supper, Dad untied me but not without a stern warning that next time I would have to stay there all night!

One day, for entertainment (since I knew better than to run away) I decided to sit by the side of the highway and throw rocks to see if I could get them all the way to the other side. That soon became dull so I spiced it up by waiting to throw until a car was coming to see if the rock would get across before the car got to where I was sitting. You can see this coming I am sure. I hit the windshield of an oncoming car and shattered the glass everywhere. The next thing I remember is being in the house under Mom and Dad's bed thinking it would protect me from my "just rewards." It did not. As I lay there, I knew Mom had invited the couple in the car to come into the house and she was examining the lady's eye to see if she could find any remnants of shattered glass. I remember wondering what in the world they would do to me or with me. I wondered if they would put kids in jail. Whatever they did to me I knew I deserved but the strange thing is, I don't remember any of the consequences except my feelings of guilt and fear. For me, that was enough! Dad would learn as I grew older that I would always be this way. Physical punishment never did anything but make me angry and more defiant. Shame and guilt was the way to go. I was a very sensitive kid, easily embarrassed, and learned many lessons that stuck with me for life as a result of it. Mom would say things to me in the spirit of teaching behavior patterns and I would listen and learn. But if I was warned, threatened, or was forced to do or not do something, guess what? I would do it (or not) or die!

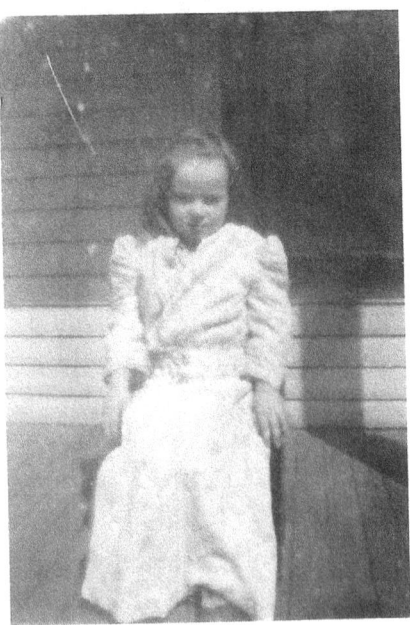

Really Getting Started

Chapter Three

Better Times Coming

It was a beautiful warm day in late summer and we were moving into a new (to us) house. I was so excited I could barely contain myself. I was almost 6 years old, would be going to school soon, and there were scores of kids in the neighborhood to play with, even a girl my age right next door who would become a significant part of my life for many years. Needless to say, I was happy about having an entire house to ourselves. No more Mrs. Dorsey!

The house was small, four rooms that made a complete circle going from one room to another. One room was quite large and the other three were quite small. I don't remember anything about how we started out but through the years we would alternate between having a living room, dining room and kitchen and one bedroom with two double beds in it for all of us. Other times we had the living room in the big room, you would come into the front door into Mom and Dad's bedroom and Karen and my bedroom was by the kitchen. Most of the time, however, the big room was Mom and Dad's and the front room was the living room. This meant you had to go through a bedroom to get to the kitchen. There was no running water, but we did have a well and a cistern of our own.

Dad always had a big garden in the summer and had to chop wood, bring in coal and kindling wood and take out ashes in winter. Not to mention putting up the "Warm morning" coal stove every fall and taking it down in spring. What a mess!

We always enjoyed the extra space we had when the stove was down. There was a huge cookstove (wood) in the kitchen that had a reservoir for heating water. It was nice to have hot water whenever we needed it but I can't imagine how hot it would have been in summer to have a fire just so they could have hot water. I was still very young when Dad brought home a kerosine stove for cooking. It was much smaller than the woodstove and gave us much needed extra space in the kitchen. I am sure Mom missed the hot water but that was progress. I won't bore my readers with the details of how things were done back then, but I want to say that I remember my parents working like dogs all the time, winter and summer. By this time in our lives we were again without a car so Dad had to walk six blocks to and from work six days a week. He worked ten hour days with one hour off for lunch (dinner in those days) and had to walk home and back for that too. I asked Mom one day why we didn't have a car because I knew we had one when we moved to Pittsfield. It was a black Ford "Model T." She said they sold it because they couldn't get tires for it. It was during World War II and lots of things were rationed. My guess would be that they didn't have the money to pay for them even if they had been available. One of the many things that were rationed was shoes. Each family received "stamps" for so many pairs of shoes according to the size of the family. Mom and Dad always laughingly told how it took most of our stamps along with Karen's to keep Karen in shoes! By this time, she was a major tomboy.

There was an old shed in our backyard, along with a privy with two concrete seats that had wooden lids. I had only seen the three holers before, like the one mentioned in the story of Mrs. Dorsey's misfortune. I thought we were right "uptown" with this newfangled one. The shed had two rooms. One was used for Dad's tools and the other was our chicken house. I remember coming home from school one day and Mom said, "go look in the shed, there is a surprise there." When I looked inside the door, there was a huge box of fuzzy yellow baby chickens! I was so excited. If I had ever seen baby chickens, I didn't remember it. I asked Mom how they got them, and she told me they came in the mail! I didn't believe her at first, but then I realized there wasn't any other way that I knew of so she must be telling the truth. I don't know how many years they raised chickens, but I remember that I couldn't stand to watch Dad chop their heads off. However, I did like to watch them flop around in the garden after he had done it! How sick is that?

After the folks decided to stop raising chickens, Dad cleaned and scrubbed the room out, lined it with cardboard, and told us it could be our playhouse. Of course, I thought it was mine and I don't think Karen ever played in it much unless I invited her. She was a tomboy and was more interested in playing with Corky (our dog) or playing outside. I was, on occasion, able to convince her to play school, or house, or office, but I was always the boss so it never lasted very long when we did play together! That playhouse is one of my favorite memories. Even as a child, I liked to have lots of time to myself and spent countless hours in that old shed by myself. It was especially wonderful when it was raining on the tin roof. The only time I ever got in trouble with the playhouse was when Dad caught me and Margie smoking dried cornsilks wrapped in toilet paper! We thought we were dead for sure, but he didn't do much but give us a talking to. He did force me to smoke one of his Lucky Strikes which didn't bother me at all, in fact I made him think I thoroughly enjoyed it. He didn't do that again but I have to admit I did smoke cornsilks and toilet paper on occasion and eventually figured out ways to snitch real cigarettes when I wanted to live dangerously.

I think it is time to introduce the girl next door who was my best friend for the next seven years or so. We thought we couldn't live without each other although sometimes we had some pretty nasty fights. It was always frustrating to me that if we had a fight and I tried to get Mom to do my fighting for me, she would have none of it! She always said, "fight your own fights. I believe if parents stay out of it, the trouble will be over and forgotten much quicker." She was right, of course. Only one time did she intervene and that was to apologize to Margie's mom for what I did and offer to pay the medical bills! I had told Margie to "get out of my yard." She said, "I don't have to." I threw a stick of kindling wood at her, never dreaming I would hit her. It struck her just under her eye and she had to get stitches and a patch over her eye. In those days they did not stitch kids up unless it was a pretty bad cut. I can't tell you how embarrassed I was at school the next few days. Margie was getting all this attention..."what happened to you?"...She was only too delighted to tell them that "Connie threw a stick at me and I have stitches in my eye." That was the first and last time I ever threw anything at anyone, having learned that the consequences could be devastating!

Margie was a good kid who led a rather unhappy life. I won't go into detail but it was anything but normal. There were dark stories about her family's past involving the murder of her "dad" at the age of 35 in an attempt to disarm a man who sought and killed the mother of a woman he wanted to marry. I learned much later he was not her biological father. She lived with the shame of her mother's lifestyle and the bitter resentment of an older sister who reminded her almost daily that she was not really her sister. Margie and I had a lot more fun times than bad ones but in thinking back, I did a lot of things without her and never wondered why until now. I went swimming a lot and don't remember her ever going with me. I skated a lot and she didn't. I went to Sunday school and she didn't. I realize now that even though we had no extra money to speak of, her family had nothing. I would guess her mother was on public aid. There were six kids when the dad died and two more kids born after he died. Margie was one of the latter. Years later I learned that her whole life had been affected, especially by her older sister's brutal mental abuse, telling Margie almost daily that she was not her sister. Ironically, the older sister ended up in a mental institution for over ten years of her adult life. One of the older sister's daughters would later become my daughter's best friend. When Margie and I finished seventh grade, her mother moved the family to Alton, IL and we have only seen each other three times since then.

I loved school! Couldn't wait to start and was thrilled that the school building was just across the road. I loved all my teachers except one who dared to discipline me one day. She was notoriously cross and didn't really like kids in my opinion. She was an old maid, I was told, but I had no idea what that had to do with anything. The rest of my teachers were wonderful and I have special memories of each one of them. Some of the memories didn't come until I was an adult and mature enough to appreciate the contributions they had made to my life. Mrs. Barkley, my first-grade teacher was one of my favorites. She made you feel like you were special to her. It became my lot to take care of her when I worked as a nurse's aid. She was dying of cancer and I had to bathe her and care for her. It was very difficult for me. I was young and learning things I did not want to know. Miss Fudge was the one I didn't like. Mrs. Martin had pretty fingernails. Miss Peecher became Mrs. Browning while she was my teacher. Mrs. Carnes and Miss Harpole were fifth & sixth grade teachers and Minna Bauch was the principal.

It was rumored that Miss Bauch had a paddle with holes in it and I made it my business never to find out. I remember my mother saying that the good thing about Miss Bauch was that she treated everyone the same. She did not favor the rich kids over the poor. One day she examined us all for head lice and some had it so we all got sent home. That was as close as I ever got to her and as close as I ever wanted to be. When my two youngest boys took the job of mowing her yard twenty-five years later, I was delighted to learn that she was a sweet little lady who dearly loved kids and teaching.

I was always glad to do my schoolwork and was conscientious about it. I would worry about how I was going to learn some things, such as writing instead of printing. I couldn't imagine how they would go about teaching me that. I never got into much trouble at school and when I did, I knew I deserved it. I could never stand seeing anyone else get into trouble either. One day when I was in fourth grade, a boy got a spanking in front of the class. He really had been bad and disrespectful, but I couldn't stand it anyway. I put my head down on the desk and my hands over my ears. I didn't even want to hear it. However, I decided to take a peek. The teacher had him by the arm and was trying to hit him on the seat of his pants while he ran in circles around her laughing. I decided it was funny and so did everyone else! I don't remember if he got sent to the principal's office or not!

It was always exciting to me when it was time for school to start in the fall, but I also looked forward to summers and being free to do as I pleased, within reason and after my chores were done. We (Margie and I and sometimes others) did everything from explore the fields, hills, hollers, creek beds, and a trash dump near our house to making cookies or pie crust in someone else's kitchen. I didn't allow this in my mom's kitchen because I didn't want to clean up the mess and I knew I would most certainly have to.

We did quite a bit of visiting in the summertime. Dad had been able to buy a car, probably from Mr. Gray's Chevrolet Garage where he worked, and our family outings involved visiting relatives. Karen and I had a lot of fun with all our cousins on both sides of the family. We grew up together like one big happy family with a whole bunch of surrogate parents. Our relationships were so different than they are for our kids and especially our grandkids. I have a lot of happy memories of good times with Mom's family but the biggest share of the memories are with Dad's family. I always went to "Granny Bide's" for at least a week in the summer. More if l could swing it! From what I have learned since becoming an adult, she was a much bigger pushover with her grandkids than she was with her kids. (What Gramma isn't?) I don't remember her losing patience with me except a couple of times. I just felt surprised that she did and I knew I deserved it. I even was conscious that I was testing her on one of those occasions.

Sometimes I would get bored at the house with Granny Bide and go to the blacksmith shop behind the house to watch Grandpa work. I remember Uncle Bill working there once. He sharpened lawn mowers for Grandpa to make some spending money. He also milked their cow which was the source of the rich cream Granny Bide would turn into that delicious "cow butter" she spread on homemade bread for me. That was a treat and a memory made in heaven. Grandpa was a little formidable to me but that was because I didn't really know him. He was a quiet man and a hard worker. I loved to sit and watch him work but I made sure I never got in his way. I would either sit on a 4 X 4 that was in the doorway of the shop or on a horseshoe keg. I watched him shoe a horse one day and couldn't imagine being brave enough to get that close to a horse and then drive nails in its hooves. I didn't get to see that more than once or twice because he did it mostly in winter. The shoes helped the horses to walk on frozen ground and ice without slipping. I would think it would help protect their hooves too.

Mostly what I watched Grandpa do was sharpen plowshares. It was awesome to me. He would hold that big piece of steel with tongs over a blazing fire. When the metal was glowing red, he pounded it into the shape he wanted it (sharp) and then dip it a big wooden tub of water called a "slack tub." This was to temper them, whatever that means. All I know is it made a most exciting sizzling noise that I can hear in my head to this day. Years later he invested in an electric hammer to do the pounding for him. It was a huge piece of equipment that I am sure saved him many hours of hard labor. It was so loud you could hear it a block away. One day he got the forefinger of his left hand caught in it and nearly lost that finger. It was totally stiff for the rest of his life. He was fortunate that he didn't get hurt worse than he did.

Sometimes Granny Bide would give me a list of things she needed from the store. She would tell me to go show it to Grandpa and he would give me the money to go uptown and buy the things for her. It was always a treat to go to Mr. Adamson's store because he seemed to like kids and would almost always let me pick out a treat for myself. I never even wondered if he was giving it to me or if he was charging Grandpa for it! Then I would stop at the shop and give Grandpa his change before delivering the groceries to Granny Bide.

I spent a lot of time at Aunt Helen's house every summer. Two or three weeks if Virginia and I could pull it off. We were as close as sisters. Probably closer because we didn't have to live together all the time! I could write a whole chapter on the good times we had and there was only one time there was a little problem between us. I'll give you just one guess who was at fault! I did something mean that I thought would be funny. It wasn't. All Aunt Helen did was was ask me "what made you do a thing like that?" I was crushed and ashamed. It was only a few moments (after she had made sure Virginia was OK) until she came to me and assured me that all was well and it was over. I had been forgiven and no one was mad at me. I don't remember ever seeing her lose her patience with any kid except once. I happened to see her chasing Ray one day with a switch in her hand, trying to spank him with it. Her tongue was sticking out as she tried to connect with his skinny little legs. I remember thinking he must have been terribly bad for her to be that mad at him!

I spent part of my summer at Aunt Helen's until I was in high school and more interested in running around Pittsfield than playing on the farm. One time, when we were pretty big kids, Virginia and I went to church camp together, which we

did more than once. This time was special though, because we played a trick on Aunt Helen that still makes me laugh....
Virginia and I had shoes alike, same size, different color...The next time our family went to visit the Guthries after church camp, Virginia and I told Aunt Helen that we sang a duet, which we did, and we both wore one shoe of each color while we sang (which we did not). Aunt Helen's reaction was more than worth telling the lie! She was shocked and seemed to swallow it hook line and sinker! We let her carry on a little and then told her it was a lie. Looking back, I wonder if she was just playing along with us.

I remember staying with Aunt Sally for a week one time. She let me take care of Genie who was only two years old, make fudge in her kitchen without worrying about any mess I might make, put up with me following her every move until one day she had to explain to me what a douche was so she could have enough privacy to go take one, and finally, she gave me a manicure set she had that I treasured the rest of my life. I know she had very few material possessions and I did not realize until I was an adult what an unselfish thing she had done. Such a precious memory! That visit was so great for me that I don't remember if I ever stayed with them again. They did the most interesting things. Aunt Sally made cottage cheese and Pete fed baby calves with a bucket that had a big nipple on it. What a sight for a city kid.

I had another Aunt Helen, but she was my great aunt, Granny Bide's youngest sister. She had two daughters who seemed like cousins to me, and I went to visit them for a few days on two or three occasions. The girls were not that much older than me and we had some good times. The girls didn't get along very well, never did their whole life, because Leona

Mae (the oldest) was mean to Mary Ruth. I was afraid not to go along with it, but I never really saw the humor in some of the things Leona said and did to Mary. Their Grandpa Crisp lived with them (my great grandpa) and I was afraid of him because the girls had told me he was mean and not to get near him. I found out years later he was not mean at all but just had to protect himself from those girls. When they weren't fighting with each other they were both picking on him and he would strike at them with his cane. He was blind, one eye totally missing, and had no other way of protecting himself Not long ago I found out he was a sweet man and it made me wish I had tried to get to know him. The story goes that Aunt Sally used to follow him around when she was a little girl asking questions about his life. He was born in Canada and she wanted to know all the circumstances of how he ended up in Pike County, Illinois! That would have been interesting. There is probably a record of some of those stories in Aunt Sally's things. She passed away and the whole family misses her terribly. She was jolly all the time and always made you feel her love and compassion.

Granny Bide

Mom & Dad's New House

Chapter Four

Growing Up

It was summer after I had finished sixth grade. I was on my way to a new life at a different school six blocks away! Exciting but frightening too. I had never been that far from home by myself except to go swimming at King Pool. The school building was much bigger than East School so the whole idea was a challenge to me. I wasn't terribly afraid, just wanted to get on with it and see what was in store for me.

Junior high was rather uneventful for me. It was very different because we had a different classroom for each subject, and I had to stay at school at noon and eat my sack lunch instead of going home. In those days there were no cafeterias. I didn't mind that at all. It made me feel even more independent. By this time, I began to notice boys and started watching my diet, wanting to lose weight. I knew I would never get a boyfriend if I stayed fat! Now, I have to listen to my granddaughters torture themselves about being fat (Karma did it too), so I guess it is just the nature of things.

Before I knew it, I was about to graduate from eighth grade. What a time for me. By this time, I had become interested in music and drama as well as school activities. I was really anxious to get into high school and become a "bigshot"! The day of my graduation, Mom had made an appointment for me to get my hair done in a beauty shop. I was excited about it but when the lady got my hair done, I couldn't believe how ridiculous it looked! Pin curls and finger waves! We did the pin curls ourselves, but the finger waves had gone out with the flapper girls of the roaring 20's. I couldn't wait to get home and hoped no one saw me on the way. As soon as I walked in the door I started combing out that hair and trying to figure out how to make it look decent. Mom said, "What in the world are you doing?" I told her I wasn't about to go anywhere looking like that, especially to my graduation. I still don't like to have my hair done in a beauty shop! I just have them cut it and let me go.

When I was about eleven years old, I asked Mom and Dad if I could start shaving my legs. They, especially Dad, said, "NO, not until you are sixteen". I always wondered why the magic number was always sixteen. "You can't shave your legs, you can't wear lipstick, you can't date until you are sixteen." Well, the day of graduation I considered myself old enough for a little defiance and after destroying the ugly hairdo Mom had paid good money for, I made the decision that I would shave my legs, keep my mouth shut and hope I got away with it. I did. In fact, Dad didn't even come to my graduation. I was a little disappointed, Mom was a lot disappointed, but I never asked why or if I did I didn't get any explanation. In those days, parents didn't have to explain their decisions, good or bad, to their children. Maybe I was just a little glad he didn't come for fear he would discover my shiny shaved legs! I remember being perfectly satisfied with my hair, my legs and my dress after having made my own decisions about all of it. Do you see a pattern beginning to develop here?

I don't remember a thing about the summer after eighth grade except how excited I was to be going to high school. We had lots of chores to do, and I had to look after Karen while Mom was at work, so it went by quickly. I had myself some fun at Karen's expense. I was mean to her and enjoyed tormenting her. However, by this time I had stopped getting physical with her because she could hurt me! I could write lots of stories about my mean behavior but one of my favorites was when I was teaching her how to pin curl her hair. She had no desire to learn, she just wanted me to do it. I thought it was time she did for herself. After all, I had learned to do mine when I was nine and she could just do the same. However, she didn't have the inclination and so it was very hard for her. The fun was in watching her try and fail and then making fun of her while refusing to help her. I probably got into some trouble for that, but if I did, I don't remember it. It's funny how I never liked to see anyone be mean to someone but I could enjoy being mean to Karen. However, I did not want anyone else to bother her. There would come a day a little later when I would even stand up to Dad on her behalf.

The summer flew by, as usual, and before I knew it, I was preparing for my first day in high school. This would be the beginning of a roller coaster ride that would last the rest of my life. Lots of good memories and bad ones as well. Memories are something no one can take away from us and I am thankful for that. I am willing to put up with the bad ones in order to have the good ones. It is strange how some things stick in your mind for no reason that you can figure out. For me, it seems like I remember the things that do not matter, and forget the things you would deem important. Karen has a much better memory than I do and I depend on her for help when I need it. It is interesting to note that for all the trouble I gave Karen growing up, she never hated me, and we have been close and a good team throughout our adult years. It seems that we compliment each other in our capabilities and the challenges of life. I have to add that there were times when I may have been justified in being so frustrated with her. She was a Total tomboy and I was Miss Priss. She told me one day that she was twelve or so before she figured out she was not one of the guys! When all is said and done, in spite of our being so opposite, we make each other laugh and get along great. If we did lose patience, we would try our very best not to ever let the other one know.

Of course, the secret to getting along is in not having to live together! Karen and I became close after I married and left home. Karma and I became close after she married and left home. Mom and Dad and I became close after I married and left home. I hope it is this way in every family. I don't like the common thread that things always got better when I was gone!

Growing Up

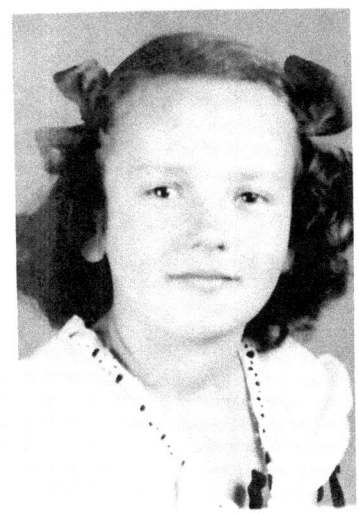

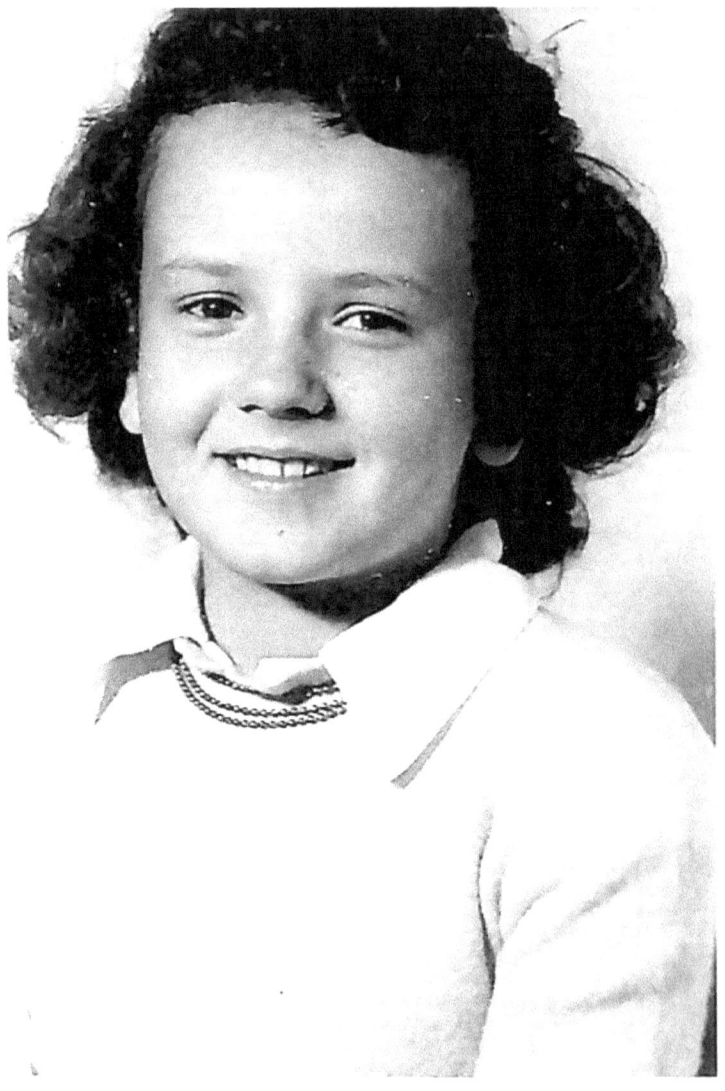

Chapter Five

High School

I don't really remember the first day of high school. I remember "Freshman Day" which was very close to the first day. The tradition has long passed away, I think, because fun gradually turned into meanness. I can't imagine what it would be like today! The tradition was that any upperclassman (junior or senior) could do anything to you they liked, and you had better do it or you could find yourself in some sort of embarrassing situation. I heard they would take some guys out in the country, take their jeans off of them, and then go off and leave them to walk home in their shorts. I never heard of anyone specifically that had it happen, but I wasn't taking any chances. The favorite things to make freshmen do were writing on their faces with lipstick, making them do "buttons"(which were deep knee bends with one hand on top of your head), or maybe pushing a rock around on the ground with your nose. Most of this silliness was forced on the guys, except the lipstick thing. I thought myself very clever when I came up with the idea of putting a thin coat of cold cream on my face to make it easier to remove the lipstick if I happened to get "initiated." I did, and the first guy was one of the Frazier boys. He noticed right away, held my arm, and yelled at everyone in sight that I needed an extra dose of lipstick for trying to be sneaky. My face was completely red, and they rubbed lipstick up and down my arms and legs until I thought I would never be clean again. It was all in fun and maybe I really wanted to make sure I got some extra attention. Who knows? At any rate, it was several days before all traces of lipstick disappeared.

High school was going to be just as exciting as I had anticipated! It wasn't long before it was time for the first football game of the year. I had a group of four girls who were my best friends and we would definitely be going to the game. (I later thought of me and my friends as the "fearsome five"!) You never saw one of us without at least one other, if not all five of us. Where the action was is where I wanted to be! I knew nothing about football itself, but I knew that anyone who was anyone would be there. I couldn't wait.

On the Friday of the first game, when school was out and I was making my way downstairs and outside to meet my friends, I noticed a boy walking down the stairs backwards and looking right at me. I knew he was a new kid in town whose dad was the manager of the Kroger store where my mom worked. I thought he was a bigshot and couldn't believe he was looking at me and smiling. He said, "Are you going to the game tonight?". "Of course," I replied. "Save me a seat, will you?" "Sure," I told him. I was dumbfounded and numb with excitement. This was going to be the first day of the rest of my life! How true that turned out to be.

Some of my friends were none too happy with me. They thought they should come first and we should all stick together. They didn't understand why I would prefer a boy over their company. That's what they told me anyway, but one of them agreed to go to the game with me and sit with me until Ralph showed up (which most of us doubted-especially me). The game was well into the first quarter when I saw him coming toward the bleachers. I had taken seats up high so I could watch for him and so he would be able to find me easily. He came right up to where I was and sat down beside me. I thought I was going to die! He explained that he had to work and that was why he was late. I was totally delighted to say the least. I didn't understand what in the world he saw in me but was absolutely thrilled with his attention. When the game was over, we made our way down the bleachers and out of the football field, managing to dodge my friend in the crowd, and proceeded toward my house. My house was at least a mile from the football field, for which I was very thankful. We walked slowly along, talking a mile a minute. I remember nothing of the conversation, just the quietness of the night and the fact that I knew this was a night I would never forget. The moon was shining as we walked along and before I knew it we were standing in front of my house. I could see that he wanted to kiss me and I made sure he could tell it was OK by me. It was the first for both of us. We probably looked like Winnie and Kevin Arnold of "The Wonder Years." After all, we were not quite fourteen years-old and neither were they.

It was love at first sight and we were inseparable the entire school year. My mom and dad felt like they were raising another kid. Dad would have liked to have had a son, but this was not his idea of how to get one! Mom thought of him as "her kid" as time went on. If it had not been for Ralph, I would have flunked Algebra. If it had not been for me, he would have flunked English. All we cared about was being together, whether we were doing homework, running around, or just sitting somewhere talking. We did lots and lots of walking because he lived on the other side of town and I loved to go to his house. To me, they were much higher on the social ladder than we were. His stepfather was my mom's boss, his mom didn't have to work, they had a bathroom and a phone, etc. It was wonderful for me too, because they didn't look down on me in any way and they acted like they loved me to death. I think they really did.

In February our school always had a Sweetheart Ball. Ralph and I made our plans to go and I couldn't wait to go shopping for a dress. I don't remember for sure where we bought it, but Mom took me shopping and we came home with a beautiful pink dress. It was strapless with a pink satin brocade bodice and very full net skirt over satin. It was ballerina length and when I put it on I felt like "Queen for a Day". When Ralph came to pick me up, he handed me a corsage and looked at me like I WAS Queen for a Day.

That was one of the most beautiful nights of my life. It was as if the music, the lights, the decorations were all done just for the two of us and we were the only ones there.

Life went on and so did the school year. By the time Spring arrived, the fairy tale had a few flaws. It has been so long ago I can't remember what we fought about but I do remember we fought a lot. Sometime early in the summer we broke up and the next thing I knew, Ralph was flirting around with another girl and even though I was so jealous I could hardly stand it, I would go to King Pool to keep an eye on them every night. They were both lifeguards and had lots of fun swimming together during "all out" time. Even though I was in pain, I developed a crush on another boy from Griggsville. He was an avid sports player and he noticed me too. The only problem was, we were both on the rebound and really weren't very nice to each other. When Ralph noticed I was flirting with someone, he lost interest in the other girl and came after me again. He assured me he was not flirting with her, but I never did believe it. We were not able to work out our differences that summer or during the entire sophomore year of high school. To my dismay, another girl was in the Sweetheart Ball Fairy Tale that year and I was reduced to going with my four girlfriends! I conned Mom and Dad into a new dress anyway and this time it was a yellow strapless dress that was all lace. I went out with lots of guys during my sophomore year but none of them meant anything to me. A lot of them simply got to walk me home one time and that was it! No one measured up. None of them were Pittsfield guys either. Ralph told me years later that it was because if he found out someone was interested in me, he threatened them and told them to stay away from me. What a revelation! I was never able to figure out why he thought I was so wonderful and not one other guy from my school agreed with him. The thing he did that made me the craziest was when he decided to "go" with someone it was usually one of my closest friends or at least someone I knew quite well. I guess you could say we were playing games.

Sometime during the summer between my sophomore and junior year in high school, Ralph and I got together and really made a go of it. It was during this time that his mother and stepfather had a baby girl. We were sixteen years-old and I could not believe anyone as old as his parents would have a baby! We thought that baby was the sweetest thing that ever happened and were quite willing to babysit her whenever we got the chance. She was a spoiled little thing and we soon found out that holding her was all you could do. Even for a baby lover like me that got old very quickly. Lucky for us, her parents didn't go out very often. She was so spoiled she slept in her parents' bed with them until she was six years old! One time her dad teased her about taking her parents with her on her honeymoon! I have lots of happy memories of being in that house with them and feeling like part of the family. Ralph, by his own admission, loves my mother to this day. It is at this point I wish the story had a different ending, but that is not to be.

Ralph and I made a go of our relationship all the way through our junior year right up until prom time. We had a big fight and broke up. He asked someone else to the prom and I ended up going with my girlfriends again. I remember that I wore the yellow dress from last year's Sweetheart Ball. What difference did it make if I didn't even have a date? It didn't turn out all that bad though. One of my friends, Bev, had invited one of my old boyfriends and he danced with me more than he did her. I felt bad for her, but I was definitely wanting Ralph to think he was my date! I never thought to ask him if he thought that or not. He probably would have pretended not to notice anyway.

During that summer after our junior year, I dated several guys and ended up going steady with a guy from Barry. We had loads of fun, but I knew I could never love him. He was already out of school and was a truck driver. His parents were in ill health and he practically supported them. Therefore, he did not own a car and had to depend on other guys to bring him to see me. Most of the time it was a guy who was so ugly he could never even dream of having a date, not to mention a girlfriend. We took terrible advantage of him. Most of the time it was Ike and me with him as well as two or more of my friends, Donna,

Rokita, Bev, and Trudy. Poor guy was in love with Rokita and we led him to believe we could get him a date with her so he would take us places and pay the bills for all of us. We were so *bad!* None of us would even skate with him (most of the time we went skating). The poor guy was either stupid or desperate, maybe both. I know the joke was that it took him three or four years to finish a six-month business course at Quincy Business Academy. You would think I would want to leave this part of my story out for shame, but not me. It was awful and I admit it, but I like remembering how much fun we had laughing about the whole thing.

Somehow during this time of hilarious fun, Ralph managed to get himself engaged to a girl from Hannibal. I never found out how that happened but I remember her name. I couldn't stand it. One night, when Ike was gone and I was running around having a ball, I ran into Ralph at the Cardinal Inn (our stomping grounds), and started a conversation with him. I announced my pending marriage to Ike (which was the farthest thing from my mind) just to get his reaction. It was just as I hoped it would be. He told me he would not allow it! I said, "there is nothing you can do about it...besides...you are getting married anyway!" "You will see," was his reply. I walked away from him acting indignant when inside I was so happy I could have died! I *knew* he still loved *me*! Prom came and went. This time I had a date with good old Ike and a new white dress that was beautiful. However this story came out, I felt like I had had the last word. My mother always said I had to have the last word and she was right. On the day we were going to practice for graduation, they told us to ask whoever we wanted to be our partner for marching in to the ceremony. I walked up to Ralph and asked him if he would be my partner. My heart was pounding so hard I barely heard him say "do you really want me to?" I said " yes" and it was settled. Later his stepdad, Walt, laughed and said I looked like the cat that ate the canary when we walked out of there! I knew very well that Ralph's fiance was sitting with his folks and I knew Ike was watching too. I didn't care.

*4 of the "fearsome 5", taken at the "Bird" in 1955.
(The Cardinal Inn, still in business to this day. Me?
I'm the one with the big mouth!")*

High School

Chapter Six

Real Life

It was summer and I was free. The problem was that I didn't know what I was going to do with the rest of my life. One day my cousin Virginia and I were together and she told me she had gotten a job in Hannibal at a furniture store as bookkeeper. She wanted me to move over there with her, get a job and share an apartment with her to help with expenses. We both knew we would have a blast, being free from home, parents, etc. to do as we pleased with no one to answer to. I was reluctant for two reasons. The big reason was, she had a job, and I didn't. I had no idea how to go about finding a job or apartment in a "city." The second reason was, she had just started dating a guy named George who wanted to be with her all the time. He had a job and a car making this possible. I had a boyfriend but he didn't have a car and I was afraid of being left alone in an apartment with nothing to do while she had places to go and things to do. She assured me that they had only been out a couple of times and she didn't think it was going to amount to anything. I finally agreed to go to Hannibal with her one day to look for an apartment, still not promising her anything. She found an apartment within walking distance of downtown and signed the agreement to take the apartment. In those days you didn't have to pay a deposit to hold a place. If so, we would have had our plans squelched right then. Looking back, this would have been a good thing. However, it was easy to trust people then and the apartment was secured. I don't remember how we came up with money to pay the first month's rent. I don't think Dad would have helped me because he was practically begging me not to go over there to live and work. It doesn't really matter anyway. I got caught up in the excitement knowing I could leave and go home anytime I wanted to, so I agreed to move over there with her even though I didn't have a job or any idea how to get one! I am not sure, but it seems to me that we used George's car to go apartment hunting and to move after we found the apartment. That should have been a big sign that their relationship was going to amount to something. I chose to ignore it and went ahead with the plan. I was fortunate to land a job at The Emporium which was a fancy women's clothing store. I was just a stock girl but was supposed to learn how to do everything including office work. I unloaded stock, priced and placed it, learned about being a salesperson (which I hated) and ran errands for the lady who ran the office. She saw to it that I never learned anything about the office work itself. I guess she was afraid I would try to take her job away from her. I hated that job! The only good thing about it was that a boy who was only fifteen worked part time as the cleaning boy and I could tell he had a crush on me. It made me feel like "an older woman" and even though I was not interested I was flattered. We would walk to the drug store together for our break time and enjoyed talking together. I was thankful he never got the nerve to ask me out because I would have hated to hurt his feelings.

By the time our rent came due the first month, I had already begun to realize I didn't make enough money to survive. Virginia and I went grocery shopping once a week and then had to carry our groceries the six blocks or so to the apartment. I was always shocked at how much the groceries cost. By the time I paid my half of the rent and groceries, I had no money left. Sometimes I couldn't even buy a five-cent Coke when I went on break. It always seemed to me that Virginia could make her money stretch farther than I could. She made a little more than me but not that much. Looking back, I wonder if George helped her a little bit.

Then I became disillusioned with the fact that Ike was not coming over to see me. We didn't have a phone, but he probably wouldn't have called anyway. He was always on the road in that stupid truck. I really didn't care if I ever saw him again, but I wanted somewhere to go and something to do. It had turned out just as I feared. George was there every night (or during the day if he was working nights) and when he came they always went out, leaving me alone in that apartment. When Virginia was home because George was working, she always had work to do to get caught up for when he would be there every night again. A couple of times we walked to the skating rink, but I usually didn't have any money. I think we went skating twice the whole summer and George went with us once! Sometimes I managed to catch a ride home on weekends but the catch was, it was with a guy who who wanted to date me and I was not interested. I had to choose between using him and feeling guilty or not getting to go home.

One weekend, in late September, feeling melancholy because I was not in school, I decided to live with the guilt and accepted a ride home with him. Then I made up a lie that I would not need a ride back. I had no idea how I would get back but if all else failed, I knew Dad would take me. He had done it before. While visiting with Mom and Dad they told me they had heard Ralph was going to go into the service. I couldn't stand it. I begged Dad to let me take his car so I could go for a ride around town. He had never let me do that but for some reason he agreed. I think he could tell I was wanting to come home for good, so he was being extra good to me.

I went straight to Ralph's house! I was in luck, he was home and very glad to see me. We rode around and talked until I had to take Dad's car home. Ralph offered to take me back to Hannibal and I was so happy I thought I was going to die. I got my stuff together and was waiting when he came after me. We got back to the apartment early and had a long time to talk before he had to leave. He never said this, but I think he was joining the service to get out of his engagement. At least partly for that reason. I made up my mind at that point that I was going to move back home where I knew I would have free room and board and an allowance for spending money, not to mention being with my friends again instead of in a lonely apartment every night. I would wait for Ralph forever if I had to! Within a few weeks and after moving back home I found out it might not be so long after all. I found out I was pregnant. I was so scared I can't tell you. I did not want to tell Dad. Ralph had left almost immediately after we had been together and I didn't know how long it would be before I heard from him or if I ever would. I felt as if my brief life was over before it had really begun.

CHAPTER SEVEN

Marriage

It wasn't long until I received a letter from him. He wanted to tell me that he still loved me and that he would be coming home on a ten day leave during the first half of November. I was so happy that I was going to see him but afraid of the news I had for him. I didn't have any idea if the idea of marriage was even a possibility, let alone a probability. I decided not to tell him until he was actually there with me in person. I was to learn later that he had made the decision not to write his fiancé a "Dear Jane" letter, but to have the decency to wait and tell her in person.

When he finally arrived, we went out riding around and he told me he had been to see her and told her the wedding was off. He said she was devastated and told him she would always love him. I felt sorry for her and told him so. Then I told him my news.

He was quiet for a few moments, thinking, and then he said "my darling, will you marry me?" The joy and relief I felt was almost more than I could bear. I asked him when we could be married and he said, "while I am home now. You will have to stay here after we are married because I have to complete six weeks of instructors training before I can get another few days off to come and get you. I will be able to make arrangements for off base living, find an apartment and then I will come and take you to Colorado with me." I could not believe that I, the country bumpkin from Pike County, was actually going to get to move to and live in Denver, Colorado. I was in heaven, not fearing anything. That is one of the many advantages to being very young. No fear.

We frantically made arrangements to be married. We had to go to Missouri to get a license and to be married because Ralph was not quite 18 and could not marry in Illinois even with parental consent. We had to go to Bowling Green to get a license and then asked a Southern Baptist minister in Hannibal to marry us in his home. My friend Trudy and her boyfriend stood up with us. We were married in front of our parents, Karen and Teija (Ralph's baby sister) on November 9, 1955. We went on a three-day honeymoon in the Ozarks and the next day after we returned, he had to get on a train in Hannibal and go to Denver. I cried for several days. It seemed like six weeks was forever!

We didn't have a car and Mom knew we needed one to get to, as well as live in, a big city. She loaned us four hundred dollars to buy an old Chevy coupe. I began gathering household furnishings, towels, sheets, dishes, etc. The apartment would be furnished, of course.

The church gave a shower for me and that helped tremendously. Before I knew it, six weeks flew by and it was time for Ralph to come get me. He had written to tell me what our address would be. 1343 Ogden St., Denver, Colorado. I was impressed!!!! The morning before we were to leave on January 1, 1956, I woke up sick. It was a holiday so Mom took me to the ER to see Dr. Shulman. He said I had a severe case of the flu and to go home to bed for a week. I said, "I can't do that. I am leaving for Denver in the morning." He looked at Mom, she nodded her head, so he gave me some really strong medicine and wished me good luck!

Early the next morning, still sick as a dog, I got in that old car with Ralph, a back seat and trunk full of all our earthly belongings, and a guy from Quincy who was hitching a ride with us. We headed West with never a look back. This was the "big adventure"! We didn't get to Barry before we had a flat tire. Ralph fixed it and we drove the rest of the way to Denver without a spare (another example of youthful unawareness of the realities of life). I was so sick all of the way that I was delirious half of the time. It was an eighteen-hour drive and we only stopped to go to the bathroom and buy gas and a cup of coffee. One time the guys had a donut, but I was so sick I didn't want one. All I wanted to do was lay down, but I couldn't because the three of us were in the front seat and the back was full of stuff. After it was all over, Ralph told me he almost turned around and took me back home because I was so sick.

I can remember the first sight of the Rocky Mountains as they came into view. What a sight, and a tumbleweed rolling across the highway in front of us as we came within a few miles of Denver. It was awesome. When we finally got to the city, we went to Lowry AFB to drop off our rider (who was supposed to pay half of the expenses of the trip the following payday, and who we never heard from again)! Then we headed for our "castle" on Ogden St. It was like a castle to me, mice, roaches, crummy furniture and all. We had running water and a bathroom, which was more than I had ever known.

However, where I grew up we didn't have roaches or mice.

I never could decide if the trade was worth it or not. We managed to carry all our stuff up the stairs, dug out some sheets and made the bed, and fell into it for about a twenty-four-hour nap. When we woke up the next day, I was surprised at how much better I felt. The medicine and the rest had done a miracle on me and I was ready to get on with our lives. We were hungry and decided the first thing to do was find a grocery store. I remember walking out on the street on January 2 in Colorado (Dad had warned me how terribly cold and dangerous the winters were and had insisted on buying me a new winter coat) wearing a sweater! It was a beautiful day. We would learn later that most of the time the winters were no worse there than in Illinois. Sometimes not as bad.

We took our groceries home and put them away, along with a big box of canned goods Walt had sent with us. We fixed something to eat and had our first meal together in our own home. Then we finished putting the rest of our things away and getting settled in. All was bliss until the weekend came. I had always been used to going to Sunday school and church and when Ralph slept until 2:00 p.m. the first Sunday we were there, I found myself feeling lonely, neglected, and maybe even a little homesick. To my surprise, I missed getting ready and going to church which surprised me because I had thought how nice it was going to be to have a choice about it. Mom never gave me a choice! If I had listened to my conscience and the tugging of the Holy Spirit, my life would have been an entirely different story. Instead, we had friends who lived in the same building with us that we spent all our spare time with. One couple was from Pike County and we had hung out together before any of us were married. The other couple was from St. Louis. We were "family" and we have been lifelong friends. Wayne and Peg live in Summerhill now and Elaine and Paul live in California, but we keep in touch. I haven't seen Elaine and Paul for 36 years. We ran around together in Denver, doing things that didn't cost money because we all were broke. We had holiday dinners together. It was a great time for all of us until I had our baby. Then things changed. We got even more strapped for money and were not free to go places. At the same time, Elaine and Peggy got jobs so they had twice as much money as we did. We gradually grew apart, but they did enjoy our baby girl when they were around.

Marriage

Finding Constance, Searching for Adventure, Finding Faith, and Everything in Between

Marriage

Chapter Eight
Babies, Bottles and Broken Dreams

The marriage went well for the first few months. Taking into consideration that Ralph and I were still children, we felt all grown up and did a good job of accepting responsibility. I knew what my responsibilities were because I had been taught at home not only what they were but how to do them. He had been taught too, and more than once he had to give blood (literally) for the ten dollars they paid for it in order to buy enough food to finish out the pay period. We didn't care. We had each other, a place to call our own, and friends to be with when we wanted to. What else is there? We would soon find out.

One day I woke up to someone knocking on the door. I was shocked to discover that I had slept until 2:00 p.m. When I went to the door, I was surprised to see my cousin Norma and her husband Bill from Illinois standing at my door. They had decided to take a vacation and come stay with us and see Colorado while they were there. In those days, you didn't bother with formalities, you just visited people whenever you felt like it. We were having a good time visiting that evening and preparing supper when I realized my water had broken! I had not packed anything to get ready for the hospital, so we hurriedly threw some things together and rushed off to Fitzsimmons Army hospital. When we arrived, the nurse took me and my suitcase behind a forbidden door and I didn't see Ralph or Norma and Bill again until after the baby was born (I envy young mothers today). I was not the least bit afraid until I heard another woman screaming "God help me" and I began to wonder what I really was in for! Karma was born on May 30, 1956.

The labor was short, just four and one/half hours from the time my water broke. However, the delivery was very difficult. It took about an hour of hard pushing to get the baby out. I would learn later, by reading it on a card fastened to the foot of my bed, that I had had a breech birth. I didn't know for years what that was. That was an army hospital for you, they didn't give you time to ask questions and certainly didn't volunteer any information. It was a frightening time for me but all worth it when I got a glimpse of that baby. They didn't clean her up or hand her to me or any of those nice caring things they do today. They just took her away after telling me it was a girl. I thought she was beautiful and looked like one of my treasured rubber dolls I had spent so many hours playing with when I was a kid. When they finally brought her to me in my room, I thought they had given me the wrong baby! Her little face was beautiful but, her head was flat on one side because of the difficult delivery. Truth be known, we were probably lucky to be alive. In this day and age they would have done a C-section. She was completely healthy, though, and I would soon learn what real love is.

I had to stay in the hospital for five days. I thought I was never going to get out of there. Ralph was allowed to come visit for one hour each evening. That was it! Once we were home, I remember how I could not believe how hard it was to get up every three or four hours at night to feed that baby. I also could not believe how precious she was and how much I loved her. It was hard work, and it soon took a toll on our immature marriage and relationship. Before very many weeks had gone by, Ralph was taking his frustration and jealousy out on not only me, but on Karma. One day she was crying while I was preparing her bottle (without a microwave it took a whole five minutes) and Ralph held her little six-week-old body up and was yelling "shut up". I cried and cried and asked him if he was ashamed of himself. He said, "no, maybe the next time I tell her to shut up she will do it." That was the worst episode I remember but there were others. However, he never did get physical with her again. The yelling got pretty bad sometimes and I was afraid a lot. One day, while Ralph was at work, I took the baby downstairs to the front porch swing and sat down to visit with the older lady who was babysitting for our landlady.

She said "Connie, are you and that baby OK?" I wanted to tell her we were not, but I didn't dare. I tried to assure her we were. She asked me a couple of times if l was sure, and I said I was, but I don't think she believed me. There were no laws back then so there wasn't much anyone could do. Besides, I loved Ralph, even though I was afraid of him sometimes and didn't want anything to happen to us.

In no time at all, I realized I was pregnant again, and I was young and foolish enough that I didn't care. We had searched and searched for a name we loved for Karma but we didn't have to do it again because we had picked out a boy's name while searching and knew we would use it if this baby was a boy. The baby was born four weeks early, on March 19, 1957, probably because I had them so close together, and though he was tiny, he was healthy. We named him Mitchell Lee, which I thought went quite well with Karma Gene, and took him home in three days. I am sure they would put him in a neonatal unit today, but back then people just had to take their chances. We were very fortunate. Had I been older, I would have been scared to death, but I was so young it didn't occur to me to be afraid. I just went about the business of taking care of two babies and it was a tremendous job. Young as I was, I did not bounce back very quickly and felt bad for a long time. Mom came out to spend as long a time with me as she could, and she would have stayed several weeks but Ralph was so irritable that she left after two weeks. The day she left we had twelve inches of snow on the ground, and it was the end of March! I will never forget that day.

It was obvious we had to get a bigger apartment and we were fortunate to know a couple who owned a house in the suburbs. He was an officer and they were from Milton, IL. Their names were Everett and Peggy Bissell. Everett was going to have to go overseas for six months and Peggy wanted to go home to Milton to stay with her parents so they asked us to live in their house rent free so we could take care of it for them. What a break for both of us. It was months before I felt normal again but having a nice little house and a few modern conveniences helped in the biggest way. It even helped our marriage relationship somewhat. The problem was six months was soon over! Thus began a series of moves from one place to another trying to find one that was suitable yet affordable. We ended up even farther out in the suburbs, but quality life was not to be had.

Before Mitch was born, I worked up the courage to tell Ralph that I was not going to endure the same kind of treatment for this baby as I had with Karma. He was none too happy with me but took it better than I had thought he would. He didn't get annoyed with Mitch until he was a year old. One night, he decided it was time to break Mitch of sucking his thumb. He laid him on the floor at his feet and every time Mitch stuck the thumb in his mouth, Ralph yanked it out. Mitch would scream, cry, and then stick the thumb back in his mouth. Ralph would yanked it out again. I yelled and threatened but it did no good. Finally, I hit Ralph and he hit me back. Then he proceeded with what HE thought was discipline of the baby. I got his rifle out of the closet and threatened him. It was at this point I made the decision to get out. I was afraid and didn't know what else to do. I knew I loved Ralph and probably always would, but I lost hope and gave up. I felt like I was living in a nightmare.

Finding Constance, Searching for Adventure, Finding Faith, and Everything in Between

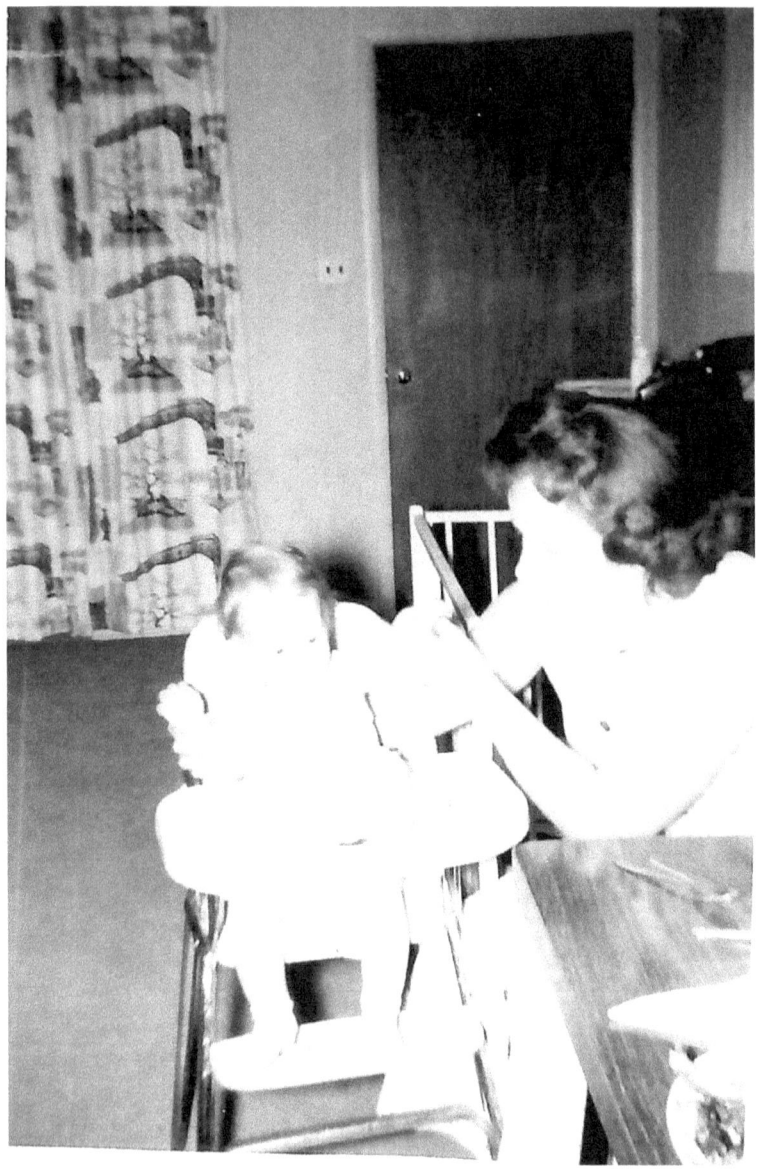

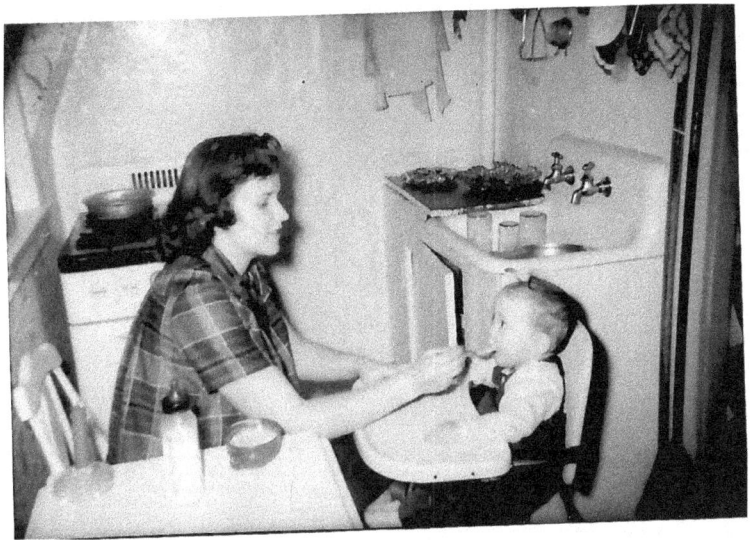

Chapter Nine

Giving Up

I don't want to imply that the entire time Ralph and I were married, things were terrible. Quite the opposite. In fact, in my older years I think about the good times much more than I do the bad times. There are so many sweet memories that I feel like I have been more fortunate than most people. We didn't have a television set so we spent a lot of time talking. We also read books out loud to each other. When we weren't fighting, we really enjoyed each other. We were just so young we didn't know how to cope with the pressures of life. We had no idea how to handle things differently. Who could at our age? However, we did what we did, and as I heard one preacher say, "You can't unscramble eggs!"

The night we had the big episode about the thumb sucking, we both realized things were getting out of hand. After I had the kids in bed, I began taking Ralph's clothes out of the closet, hangers and all, and throwing them in the back seat of the car. All the while I was yelling "I want you out of here tonight!" All the while he was begging me for another chance and after a while I calmed down enough to stop what I was doing and at least not make him leave that night. However, I despised him at that moment, and I knew things were never going to really be OK. The idea of going back to Illinois became more of a reality that night. There were other factors besides the issues with the kids and his desire to completely control me. At one point I believed he was having an affair. It didn't last long and I really didn't care except for the lying. At another time I was considering having an affair but found out I didn't have the nerve. I told Ralph I wanted a divorce for several reasons, one of them being to get away from the man who was trying to "get" me (Who just happened to be his boss on base!). I just wanted to go home where I would be safe, I thought, from all bad things. Not that I wasn't tempted. I was, but just didn't have the nerve to actually have an affair with my husband's boss. I was young but I had enough sense to know that no good could come of it. And so, after an all night discussion, Ralph rented a U-Haul trailer, put everything we had except his clothes in it, and we headed for Illinois. I didn't even let Mom and Dad know I was coming! Ralph begged me all the way home to give him another chance, and the odd thing is I knew I wanted to. But I had heard all of the promises before, many times, and my pride wouldn't let me give in.

We arrived in Pittsfield late in the evening and I told Mom and Dad what was going on. The next morning, we unloaded the U-Haul and Ralph and I said goodbye. Mom cried, I didn't. That would come later. I was in such a bad emotional state that it was affecting me physically. I was unable to function well enough to get an apartment, a job, and get out on my own. I lived with Mom and Dad for six months. I paid them ten dollars a month out of my ninety-five dollar allotment check from the USAF and kept house and cooked for them. It was very hard on all of us. I got some medical help (Phenobarbotol) and gradually got better emotionally. Then I became determined to get out on my own, with no experience, and get my own place so I could live my life my way. I didn't like Dad's opinion that I had to obey his rules just like I had when I was in high school. This was the time in my life when my independent nature really bloomed! It had always been there, but now it began to grow.

On Friday nights Karen always went skating. It was one of the things I had always loved to do and didn't expect to ever get to do again. One night, after I had the kids in bed for the night (this was one of Dad's rules) I decided to go skating with Karen. We had a ball! It became an every Friday night thing and I began to feel like I would have a life and be happy again. I also began to resent Dad's rules (be home by 10:00 p.m., for example) even more.

As soon as I got settled in with the folks, I realized I wanted to be in church again. I had never made the effort the whole three years I lived in Denver. Ralph and I had discussed it but never got around to doing anything about it. I knew I wanted my kids to have Christian upbringing the same as I had. Ralph had been raised and schooled Catholic, but he didn't want that. I think I could have made a Southern Baptist out of him if I had tried. It is recorded in my old high school diary that he went to church with me a lot when we were dating. I remember praying and praying that he would be saved but it never happened. It was too late for that now, but I got myself and my babies into church. I was determined to get everything right in starting this new life of mine. Only one problem. I had been saved when I was eleven years old and trusted God for my salvation but I had never trusted Him with my life. I was afraid He would take away something I wanted or make me do something I didn't want to do. One day, while Granny Bide was visiting us, Mom and Granny Bide were talking about their salvation and the peace it had brought into their lives. They were having a wonderful time sharing their love for Jesus. As I listened, I realized I didn't have the same kind of peace they were talking about. I believed fully and had testified to the fact that I had been saved and would go to heaven if I died, but I knew something wasn't right. I began to cry as I listened to them talk.

When they noticed, I told them what I was feeling and we prayed together. Finally, they asked me if I felt better and I told them I did. There was no emotional big deal involved. I just knew I had done all I could and renewed my determination to live my life God's way.

It was around this time that I met a man named Roderick Sanderson. He was always at the skating rink on Friday night and would skate with me most of the time. Then we began to go for car rides and spend time together. As the relationship between Rod and I progressed, I learned that he had been raised in the Christian church in Detroit, IL. He said he was a believer and I took this as a sign of God's blessing on the relationship. It was not. However, after three years of dating on and off (I had finally got my divorce a couple of years after I came home), I agreed to marry him. I knew he would work and make a living for me and the kids so I told myself it didn't matter. He would be good to us and we would have a place to live and food to eat. Also, I needed a car. Karma was starting kindergarten at South School and I lived in an apartment a mile away. I worked at Farmer's State Bank and it took over a third of my salary to pay babysitters. I was not making a living and was desperate. By this time Ralph had been discharged from the Air Force so my ninety-five dollar allotment check was a thing of the past. All of the wonderful programs they have today for single moms were non-existent back then. I couldn't even get help getting my teeth fixed, which would have been a one-time thing, let alone a monthly check and medical expenses paid. Neither did they track down dads and make them pay or go to jail. I had received two checks from Ralph and was told later that his stepdad had sent me that money. I never knew if that was true or not.

One Sunday when I got to Mom's after church, there was a big surprise waiting for me. A strange car was in the driveway and when I walked in the house, a man I didn't know was sitting on the couch. The next thing I knew, Ralph came walking out of the bathroom. I was so happy to see him I can't put it into words. We had a great visit and I would soon learn he had things all figured out. He had asked my folks if his friend could sleep at their house that night. His plan was to spend the night with me at my apartment. We talked for hours and hours. We admitted we still loved each other and decided to get things worked out and get married again. One problem. He was out of the service and had been traveling and living in his car with his friend for the past year! The plan was that he would go to Minnesota where his folks were living, get a job, and then come and get us. It sounded great to me.

Late that evening, he said, "Let's go to bed." I felt wrong about it and said so. "We are divorced," was my argument, but he told me if I didn't he would leave. I couldn't stand that idea (I swallowed it hook, line, and sinker) so I complied with his wishes. I felt used but did nothing about it.

After he left, we wrote to each other regularly, and I told Rod I was going to marry Ralph instead of him. Frankly, I was relieved, even though in the back of my mind I knew Ralph and I might not make it. I couldn't give up hope. One day I got a letter telling me he had a job and plans for buying a house. He wanted me to leave the kids with someone, get on a bus, and come to Minnesota to visit, meet his friends, etc.

Easier said than done. Mom worked, so I had no one to leave the kids with. I had no money for a bus ticket and he didn't offer me any. I had no idea how to go about buying a bus ticket and traveling to Minnesota by myself. I was afraid. When I conveyed all these reasons to Ralph, he informed me that I should have known he would reimburse me the money for traveling when I got there. He saw all my reasons as excuses. When I answered his letter, I told him he was hopeless and I never wanted to see or hear from him again. And so it was.

It wasn't long before Rod found out the whole thing was off and he started coming around again. He wouldn't leave me alone even when I wouldn't even speak to him! As I said before, my financial situation was desperate. I finally agreed to marry Rod and we set a date for October 7, 1961. Karen and Harold were getting married too, so we decided to have a double wedding. I remember the night I was getting ready for the shower they were having for Rod and me at the Detroit Town Hall. I prayed over and over, "Please God, don't let this be a mistake". How stupid is that? Telling God what I was going to do whether He liked it or not and then asking Him to bless it! I just made up my mind that no matter what, I would have to live with it for my kids' sake. After all, I had them and I owed them food, clothing, a way to school, and a roof over their heads. I knew I couldn't do it on my own. Several people tried to tell me I was making a mistake, not because Rod was a bad person, quite the opposite. He was as good as he could be, but they all knew I would be unhappy. I have never understood why people think once you are married everything will be okay whether you love each other or not. Myself included!

I would not listen to any of the warnings, including Mom's, which was kind but not the least bit subtle, so the wedding went off as planned. It was on the wedding night that I knew I had made a dreadful mistake. I had ordered a pretty nightgown (I couldn't afford) and when I put it on he looked at me and said, "where did you get that thing?" He was making fun of me and I was crushed. He took me to Chicago for a honeymoon. We visited his Aunt and Uncle in Chicago and my Aunt and Uncle on the way home (free place to sleep)! How romantic. The whole marriage was just that romantic. Not that I believe in fairy tales, but I guess I did back then. I haven't been called "Pollyanna" more times than one in my life for no reason!

Karma and Miteh

Roderick

Chapter Ten
Trying Not to Give Up

After the 'honeymoon' we got settled in the house Rod and I had rented and he had already moved me into. It was exciting to have a house instead of an apartment and Karma and Mitch enjoyed having their own room. It was good to be a family with a dad again, the financial burden was lifted, I continued to work, and I told myself I was happy. The first Monday morning Rod returned to work after the wedding, he said "bye" and left the house. I assumed he would be home for supper that evening since he had told me no different. The next time I saw him was Friday night for supper. I had imagined all kinds of things but didn't want to call his boss. I assumed if anything bad had happened, I would have heard from someone. Every day I thought he would be home that night only to be disappointed and worried again. When he finally did come home, I was thankful he was OK and told him I was worried to death. He simply said, "you knew I was a truck driver when you married me and you should know better than to look for me until you see me coming." I had never been around truck drivers and had no idea how they worked. I became angry at his uncaring attitude and let him have it. He was surprised at how mad I was but never (the whole time we were married) apologized.

I soon got used to the situation and learned not to care when he came home. He gave me the paycheck every week and expected me to take care of all business and decision making. He would mow the yard when needed and occasionally help with some cooking and that was the extent of his contribution to family life. He had always acted like he loved my kids and I had no fears of him not being a good "dad." Well, he wasn't a bad dad. He was just no "dad" at all. For years I tried to get him to communicate with me and the kids, but he just wouldn't. He nit-picked at Mitch a lot and it broke my heart.

Most of the time I kept my mouth shut because I didn't want anyone to ever be able to accuse me of not letting him be a "dad." He didn't nit-pick at Karma much because he soon learned that she would tell him off instead of just taking it. The last thing he wanted was a confrontation, even with a child!

After we had been married a year and five months, I learned I was pregnant. I really didn't want any more kids but because everyone, especially my mother-in-law, told me that it wouldn't be fair to Rod, I decided to go along with it. Secretly I hoped it wouldn't happen. Forget that! However, it didn't take long for me to get excited about the baby. It had been a long time since I had enjoyed a baby and Karma and Mitch were excited too. I am sure Rod was excited too, but of course he never said so. It just wasn't his nature.

Time went by and before we knew it, it was time for the baby to come. I was 17 days late when Vince was finally born on October 20, 1963. He weighed 8 lb. 13 oz. Rod was gone with a load of hogs to St. Louis so I called Mom. Dad stayed with Karma and Mitch and Mom and I left for the hospital at 10:35 p.m. Vince was born at twenty-three minutes after 11:00 p.m. I couldn't tell if l was in labor or not. Good thing I didn't wait any longer.

We named the baby Vincent Leland after both grandpas and both grandpas were as proud as they could be. He was a good baby, and everyone thought he was the greatest thing since sliced bread! We all spoiled him, but he wasn't the type to become spoiled. We knew before he was born that we needed a bigger house, so we looked for one and found one we liked on Dutton St. When Vince was about three weeks old, we moved. By this time Karma and Mitch, especially Mitch, (the neighborhood was full of boys) had made a lot of friends and they hated to move away. It turned out that there were plenty of friends where we moved to, more for Karma in fact, and they soon adjusted to their new life. They even had to change schools, but they adjusted to that quickly as well. I had given up my job at Farmers State Bank when I was six months pregnant with Vince (I hated the job anyway). All I ever wanted to be was a wife and mom and so, now my dream had come true. I had always wanted a two-story house, a husband, and kids. Because I wasn't working, money was very tight, so I took a babysitting job. It was a little boy who was eighteen months old and very busy. My "daydream come true" soon turned into a zoo! I found myself with more work to do than any one woman should ever have to do. The good thing was, I was so busy I didn't have time to pine about lost love and broken dreams. I was actually somewhat content for several years. Besides having all these kids and work, Mom began coming down with a nervous breakdown. She was only three blocks from me and would walk to my house every day, sit and play the piano and cry. I had lunch hour from 11:00 a.m. until 1:00 p.m every day, and then one night Vince became very sick very suddenly. He could not breathe and we had to rush him to the hospital. He was so bad they prepared him (and us) for a tracheotomy. However, they put him in an oxygen tent in a room with lots of moisture and it seemed to ease his breathing. Dr. Bunting said, "You have a very sick baby." He told us later that this was possibly one of the problems that causes infant death syndrome. We were in the hospital for a week. The next winter, when Vince was a little over a year old, he did the same thing. This time it was not so severe, probably because he was older and stronger.

One day, when Dad was home, he called me and told me we had to do something with Mom. I said, "What do you mean?" He said, "She does nothing but cry and won't get up off the couch. We have got to do something now before we both go crazy." I called Dr. Barrow and he made an appointment for her with a psychiatrist in Quincy. He told us they would probably put her in the hospital. When I told her, she said, "I will see the doctor but I am not staying in the hospital!" She did. When we left the doctor's office Dad said to me, "What should I do?" I told him to drive to the hospital. Mom said she would not get out of the car, but she did. From that day on, I felt like they depended on me to do all of that kind of thing for them. I was twenty-six years old. Mom was forty-five years old.

Mom had an extended stay in the hospital. They gave her shock treatments (the maximum) and finally sent her home with medication. They called her illness "menopausal depression." She gradually got better but it took a long time. Then when she was fifty years old she took swimming lessons and learned how to dive off the high board after being scared to death of water her whole life. That same summer she took classes and earned her GED. In the fall of that year, she entered nursing school and became an LPN. She made straight A's and was asked to speak at her graduation ceremony. I was as proud of her as she would have been of me if I had done something that great. After graduation, she worked at Illini Hospital for ten years and enjoyed every minute of it.

In the meantime my family life was marching on. We decided to buy an old shack on the other side of town at the urging of Rod's parents. It was driving them nuts that we were "wasting money paying rent." We couldn't afford a decent place and had no down payment. The house was stuck in an estate and they were desperate to sell it, so the bank was willing, not only to sell it to us with no down payment, but loan us extra money to fix it up. I had never heard of, and never have since, a bank sticking their neck out that far.

However, I had worked there and they knew we were a good risk. After we got in there I understood why they were so helpful. No one else would have been crazy enough to buy it unless they had the money to bulldoze it and put up a new one! It seemed like the harder we worked the worse it looked.

We lived there four years and I hated every minute of it. The house was so small we were cramped. It looked so shabby I was ashamed of it, and by this time Vince was on his feet and running, busy every minute. Karma had always been such a sweet and loving little girl, but about this time she started having some pre-puberty symptoms. Put that together with a little brother who was into everything she had and she developed an attitude problem. If it hadn't been for her friend, Juanita (who was my childhood friend Margie's niece), and their Barbie dolls, I don't know what I would have done with her.

She never went out and did bad things, she just got pouty and sassy and nothing I could do pleased her. We couldn't agree on anything.

Mitch had several friends in the neighborhood and was having lots more fun than I ever dreamed of. Most of it was innocent fun, but he got into a couple of pretty serious scrapes. One day a contractor, who was building a new house in the next block, came knocking on my door. To make a long story short, Mitch and his friends had made a very nasty mess in the man's partly constructed house. They had thrown mud, rocks, and who knows what else all over it. He was especially upset about the kitchen cabinets he had just finished. I told him we had no money, but if he wanted Mitch to clean it up, he was more than welcome to make him do it. He said, "no, it would be easier to do it myself".

One day the phone rang and it was the mother of one of Mitch's friends. She asked me if Mitch had a bunch of new pocket knives. I told her "no." She told me to go look in his underwear drawer. Guess what. I found two or three lovely brand new pocket knives hiding under his shorts! When I confronted him, he made no effort to deny it. Of course, it was all Mike's fault, not his, he didn't want to do it, he just did it because the rest of the guys wanted to. I marched him straight to Ideal Hardware and made him give the knives back to Mr. Hass. I encouraged Mr. Hass to "talk" to Mitch and he did. We were both crying when we left the store. I thought I had taken care of that situation quite nicely. I was to learn years later that I hadn't changed a thing!

I mentioned Vince being busy. That is putting it mildly. He wasn't mean or mouthy, just into everything. I felt like I had to do everything twice. He also bothered the neighbors but it wasn't his fault. He was just a typical two-year-old. One day he was playing so nicely I couldn't believe it. It was a little too quiet. Come to find out, he had found a screwdriver and removed most of the doorknobs in the house! Another day, he was playing outside and every little bit I would yell out the door "Vince!" "What, Mamma?" "What are you doing?" "Playing." "Stay in the yard." "OK, Mamma." This went on for an hour or so. Pretty soon, the neighbor, Mr. Hurd, knocked on the door.

When I answered he told me Vince had the top off an old cistern we had in the yard by the corner of the house! It probably had six feet of water in it and he had thrown every toy, stick, rock, and flowerpot in it that he could find! I won't bore you with more stories like this, though there were many. It is why I am convinced that every little boy and girl is blessed with a guardian angel from God (moms too!).

I know the kids had some good times while we lived in that old house. There were lots of kids around to play with. There were also some neighbors who were older, impatient, and caused us some grief. Of course, the kids caused their share of the grief as well. All the kids, not just ours. They were all just kids and the old folks were old folks! The kids didn't know the house needed lots of repairs, the yard was mowed but not really well taken care of, nothing ever got done to the cars or that their mother was a very unhappy person. I worked hard all the time, even on weekends, keeping the house spotless, taking care of three kids, making all the decisions, and taking care of all family business. Life as I knew it became unbearable to me. I remember one Sunday afternoon in particular. We took a car ride (that was all we could afford to do for entertainment and was Rod's favorite thing anyway). As we rode along, I became overwhelmed with the desire to see and talk to Ralph. I was shocked to realize that I still missed him after all that time. I just stared out the car window with tears running down my face, aware that Rod knew I was crying. I couldn't stop crying and he couldn't ask me what was wrong. I finally made a quiet little plan in the back of my mind when Vince was about two years old. The plan was, to get a job, get Vince in school, eliminate childcare costs, and get a divorce. I felt like living with Rod was like having another kid to take care of. (As if getting a divorce was going to make my life any easier.) I was desperate for emotional and physical companionship that was just not to be had in this marriage. It made me feel better just to have a plan!

Plans are all well and good, if you can pull them off. Mine got foiled. I got a job all right, and after working three weeks I got pregnant. I was afraid to tell my boss because I had all but promised him I wouldn't be having any more kids. When I finally did tell him, he was not the least bit happy. He knew I was unhappy about it so he was kind in spite of his disappointment. He wanted to know if I would come back after the baby was born, but I told him I couldn't get everything done as it was and I didn't see how I could. In my mind I thought if I was going to have to stay married to Rod (which I knew I was) I was not going to do everything and help him make a living too.

I was depressed and cried for the first three months of the pregnancy, but then I found myself wondering if it would be a boy or a girl. I decided another girl would be nice and before I knew it, I realized I loved that baby with all my heart. I had always gotten the gender of my choice so felt pretty sure of myself that it would be so again. By the time my due date came close, I could hardly wait! I continued working at the bank until two weeks before the baby was due. It was December 14, 1966 when Troy Roderick was born. I had worked all day and then attended Karma and Mitch's Christmas program at Higbee School. When I walked in the door at last at 9:30 p.m. that night, my water broke. It was interesting that as sure as I was that I would have a girl, I could never come up with a girl's name I really wanted but never had any doubt about what I would name a boy. I have to say here that, when Mom told Karma she had another baby brother, she said, "Oh shit." She was really fed up with Vince's tricks and assumed Troy would be no better! Karma didn't show Troy near the attention she had shown Vince when we brought him home. I don't recall that Mitch did either, but Vince did, and I did.

Vince was my constant companion and "helper." It was obvious that he dearly loved his baby brother. One day, the baby was crying and I was busy in the kitchen. Before I could get to the crib, Vince came walking out of the bedroom with Troy in his arms and said, "don't worry, Mommie, I have him!" He had climbed up the side of the crib, picked Troy up, and climbed back down without dropping him. I could never imagine how he managed that. I calmly (on the surface) told him to put the baby on Mommie's bed. He did so and I took over from there. I had a flashback to the time I took care of Karen when I was four years old and thought I was being a big help. It was almost an exact repeat performance. Vince continued to "take care of" his little brother until Troy got old enough to tell him to stop it!

Another memorable moment in time occurred when Karma came home from school one day and told me she was sick. As it turned out, she had the mumps. When she was beginning to feel somewhat better, after about a week, all three of the boys developed a fever within days of each other, and guess what... so did I! Karma was ten, Mitch was nine, Vince was four, Troy was ten months, and I was thirty years old. Talk about doing things with your kids. This was ridiculous! I remember Mom telling me I was going to be really sick if I didn't stay in bed. I told her I would do that if she could tell me how when I had four sick kids. It turned out that none of us were terribly sick, but I worried about the boys having complications that could affect the rest of their lives. As for me, the worst part was the pain in my jaws and neck caused by the swelling. We lived through it and were none the worse for wear.

Troy grew like a weed and by the time he was two years old, we were in desperate need of a bigger house. I was glad because I hated the house we were living in anyway.

I began keeping my eyes and ears open for the house of my dreams. One day I happened to drive down Kellogg St. and saw that a big old house I had always loved was for sale. I had been in it briefly right after Rod and I were married and knew that someday I wanted a house just like it. It had eight rooms, two baths, a walk-in closet, a barn out back that would serve as a garage and an acre of land for the kids to enjoy. I decided I had to have this place regardless of what it took to get it. I found out that Farmers Home Administration was the owner. The house had been repossessed from a couple who had moved off to Kansas City and then ended up divorced. It had been sitting empty for a year and was a total mess. I didn't care! I knew it was going to be our home and I went to war to get it. It took months of camping on the doorstep of the FHA office, pleading with the man in charge, downright making a nuisance of myself until I finally talked them into bending the rules so we could have the house. The biggest rule was, they were not supposed to finance a house for someone who already owned a house. That man actually came to see the house we owned and agreed that we needed a bigger house. I'm sure if they had found another prospective buyer, I would have lost my war, but they did not and I prevailed! I am so thankful to this day.

Chapter Eleven
Moving to the Big House

After months of hope and then despair, Rod and I finally met with the people from Farmers Home Association on a Sunday. It was the only time we could all get together because one of them lived in Kansas City. We signed all of the necessary papers and I, at last, had the key to my dream house in my hand. I know everyone but me was worried about how we would handle two house payments. I didn't care how we would do it. I just knew we would. As it turned out, when we were finally ready to move, we rented the old house to a couple who lived there until we sold it and they paid their rent promptly every month. We finally sold the house to a couple who enjoyed fixing up old places, (I thought, "lots of luck") for just exactly what we owed against it. We lost money on it, but I considered it fortunate that we were able to unload the place! This did not take place for over a year after we had moved to Kellogg St. By that time I knew for sure I had not made a mistake in fighting for the house I had wanted so badly.

The first time I walked inside the big house to actually start cleaning and getting ready to move, Mom was with me. Troy was too, of course, and years later he told me that it was his first childhood memory. He has no recollection of the old place on Grant Street. Well, it is a good thing Mom was with me because that kitchen was full of cobwebs and big old bags of spider eggs! I loved this house, but not enough to walk into that mess.

We had mops, buckets and brooms with us and Mom said, "Oh here, give me that broom!" I gladly did so, and she attacked that spiders' paradise with a vengeance! I watched her until I became ashamed of my cowardice and joined in the "fun". We spent hours every day getting that place cleaned up and livable. One of the rooms upstairs had been a kitchen at one time. In fact, the whole upstairs had been an apartment. We needed to get rid of the kitchen and make it into a bedroom for Mitch. It was the only room in the house we did any repairs to. We patched and painted and scrubbed with the help of a friend of ours until that room looked as good as the rest of the house. All the rest of the house received was a thorough scrubbing and cleaning.

At last I was ready to buy and hang curtains. But before that was done, I needed to take care of the yard. We got possession of the house in late summer and the yard hadn't been mowed all season. It was more than knee high and nothing but weeds. I had to do that job with a push mower and I worked like a dog getting it done. I don't remember anyone helping me or even noticing my hard work. I was beginning to feel some really bitter resentment about the fact that I had to do everything myself (without help from my husband) if I wanted anything done. It is a shame how Satan can take the joy out of the good things in life by fooling us into concentrating on the bad.

The day came at last when Mom and I began the enormous job of hanging curtain rods and curtains at each of the sparkling clean 30 windows in that big old house. Every time we went over there to work, I also took as many boxes of stuff with us as we could, and we would put it all away before leaving for the day. As well as I can remember, I think it took us about a week to complete the curtains. One day I was there alone working when the man from Farmer's Home Association came by to see how I was doing. He wanted a tour of the house and was very complimentary about how hard we had worked and how nice everything looked. Then he wanted me to show him the barn. I thought that a little strange and a little red flag went up in my head. I showed him the barn and kept my distance as he would "accidentally" step a little too close to me for comfort. It was at that moment I think I understood just a little better why he had been so willing to bend rules for me. I was shocked at the idea of his desire to make a pass at me. The incident passed without anything happening, but I never got over the idea. Years later his wife divorced him because he was caught having an affair! Then I knew for sure it was not my imagination. Whatever the case may have been, I was happy to get my "dream" house at last and could hardly wait until it was time to actually move in. After much hard work and eager anticipation, we were finally ready to move.

The day we moved was partly cloudy and threatened rain all day, but we got almost everything moved before we actually got rain. The rain came when we were moving all the mattresses! I didn't care. I was going to sleep in that house that night. I did. Of course, the mattresses are the last thing you move so I was finished with that old house on Grant Street except to clean it up and give the keys to our renters. In some ways I feel like my life didn't really begin until I got that big house. Of course, it was really right in the middle of the busiest time of my life. I know that old house was ugly to some people, but it had the potential of really being the house of my childhood dreams. One room had the ugliest wallpaper I had ever seen or ever would see! At first glance the design reminded you of pine trees. I didn't care. I had grand expectations of transforming it into something wonderful.

We settled in gradually and the kids were happy with their new bedrooms. Karma and Mitch had a good-sized room to themselves, and Vince and Troy were glad to share the biggest room. Troy was about to turn three years-old and we were finally getting him out of his crib and into a twin bed. We had rented the barn to a friend of ours named Donnie Guthrie and he kept quarter horses and a pony out there. I had the best of both worlds and so did the boys. They had a blast riding the pony and I didn't have to pay the feed bills or the vet bills! One day Donnie told me he was going to have to get rid of the pony. It had foundered and needed to be put out of its' misery. He pointed out the upturned hooves to me and said that was how he could tell what had happened. I told him he would have to tell Vince and Troy because I didn' t have the heart. I knew they would be devastated. When they came in the house later and told me Donnie was getting rid of the pony, they didn't seem all that upset. Sorry to give up the pony but not like they knew it was going to the "glue factory." It turned out that Donnie had doctored the story a little and told them he had given the pony to a smaller child. He told them it was hard on the pony for them to ride it because they were getting so big. That was true, of course, but there was no smaller child and he left out that part. Pretty good thinking, I thought.

Before too long I began to realize that I had no choice but to go back to work. The kids were getting older, Karma and

Mitch were in junior high, Vince was going into third grade and Troy would be in kindergarten in another year. I didn't want to go back to work! I decided that beauty school was the answer for several reasons. My goal was to own and operate my own shop at home so I could be there with the kids. They were too old for a babysitter and too young to leave alone. I had always had an interest in doing hair...gave a lot of home perms and haircuts to family members. I figured if I had to work, I would at least get to do something I liked. And, if I was going to do hair, I might as well get paid for it. I remembered seeing beauty shop bank deposits of sizeable amounts when I was working in bookkeeping at First National Bank. I made the decision that I would go for it.

I mentioned the idea to a close friend of mine and was surprised to learn she had been thinking the same thing. We made plans to check into it and see what we could do. It was the beginning of a hard time for all of us, but I believed it was the right thing for the whole family. I still believe it was, though I look back and wonder how we made it through. Donna and I knew it would save us both lots of money to share driving and it was a good thing we did. The week we drove my car, Emmett, her husband, would work on hers. The week we drove her car, Rod would have to get someone to work on mine. We only broke down twice...once in my car and once in hers. If I remember right, we both had to trade cars after we graduated from school. We didn't care. We thought we were going to be rich anyway!

We went to visit the school to find out everything we needed to know, mostly how much money we would have to get and how to get it, and went forward with our plans from there. We scheduled ourselves to begin classes on October 1, 1970.

We obtained federal loans to finance the actual fee the school charged. The loans were low interest, and you didn't have to start paying them back until nine months after you graduated. I couldn't believe how well things were coming together.

Having the money to pay my tuition at school was the easy part, however. Money to drive back and forth and for other unexpected expenses was going to be a problem. We were barely able to keep the bills paid as it was. Rod was not happy with me for getting this big idea. He asked me how I thought I was going to pay for it and I told him I would figure out a way. I did. How this happened I don't remember, but I ended up with a job at Pine Lakes restaurant for the summer. I had always thought I would despise working in a restaurant and I was right. First of all, the place was only meant for the Pine Lakes campers to get a quick snack occasionally. The people in Pittsfield are so deprived of good places to eat they will try anything. Therefore, Dr. Shaw (the owner) had his hands full. Every entrepreneur's dream! He was not equipped for the thriving business he acquired in a very short time and the dream took on the characteristics of a nightmare! I was hired to cook, which I knew I could do. I told him I did not want to wait tables.

Well guess what? Half the time I had to do both. I later spent the greater part of my working years as bookkeeper and teller in a bank and I am still of the opinion that it takes less brains to do that than be a waitress.

At home things were rough. Karma had just graduated eighth grade and I gave her the job of finishing and serving supper to the family every evening. I would plan and start the meals and she (with Rod's help, he was good about that) would get everyone fed and the mess cleaned up. During the time she was having to do all this she was also babysitting for a couple of hours until Rod got home from work. I know it was hard on her, but it was going to get even worse once I was in school. Looking back, I realized that I should have given Mitch more responsibility. The only reason it was probably a good thing I didn't is because he and Karma fought so badly. Probably best I kept them separated. I found out years later that she had regrets about some of the things she did to the boys...especially Vince. She even apologized to him after they were both grown!

Looking back, I find it interesting that they didn't tattle on her. Maybe they told it all to Rod. He would never have done anything about it or told me about it. If I had known what all was going on I probably would not have gone through with my plans.

In order to save the money I was making (which was just a pittance) for expenses, I told my mother I was going to give it to her every week. She told me she would match whatever I gave her. It had always been her dream that I would get some kind of "higher education," and she wanted to encourage me every way she could. I have no idea how much money I ended up with, but it was enough to get me through. Before I knew it, the summer was over and it was time to get the kids in school (all but Troy who was only four years old) and get on with the big adventure.

Donna and I worried a little about bad weather and driving every day but for the most part, we couldn't wait to get started. It was going to be even more fun than we had anticipated. For me, I enjoyed the driving time in the mornings because I needed time to get relaxed after the mad race of getting the kids ready for school. I had to leave at 7:00 a.m. and a dear friend of mine came and got my kids and kept them until time for school. She kept Troy all day and she had four kids of her own! I don't think I ever thanked her enough for all she did for me. She would just have said "don't be silly" anyway. The driving time at night was good too, because it gave me time to unwind and get ready for the action at home. Karma started supper every night with Rod's help, and they would have it ready when I got there. I was gone eleven hours a day, five days a week.

Pencil sketch of the "Big House" artist Connie Leahr

Chapter Twelve
The Big Adventure

At last the day came, we were actually going to start classes. We had already been there several times and were familiar with the building, parking facilities, and the teachers. We had gotten over any anxiety we felt and were ready to get down to business. We had no idea how much fun we were going to have along the way. We also had no idea how hard it was going to be to take care of our responsibilities at home and do the work required to get through this and prepare ourselves to pass state board exams. Donna and I had been friends since eighth grade and had always enjoyed each other, so we knew we would get through it and have a good time doing it.

Miss Julieanne was the senior instructor. She was a very dignified older lady who turned out to be very funny also. We loved her to death. The other instructor's name was Miss Brenda. She was our teacher. The first time I saw her I could not believe my eyes. She was the tallest and biggest woman I had ever seen. At the time I was thirty-three years old and was shocked when I learned Miss Brenda was only twenty-two. She was jolly and intelligent and a very sensitive person. She had never had a date but dreamed of marrying and having a family. I've often wondered if that ever happened. I always wished there was something I could do to make her dreams come true.

The owners and operators of the school were Mr. Jim and Miss Pat. They were married and most of the time he wasn't there, but Miss Pat was the third instructor when one was needed. She was lots of fun too, just one of the girls, and we would learn later that she was a Christian. There were two classes. A large one that had begun on September 1 and ours, there were five of us, that had started October 1. We had class all morning and then worked all afternoon in their huge beauty shop. The first thing they taught us was how to give a good shampoo. If you don't get a good shampoo when you get your hair done, you don't feel like you've been to the beauty salon.

I won't bore you with any more details of school except to say that in nearly ten months of driving our old cars every day we only broke down on the road twice. Once in Donna's car and once in mine. The rest of the time it was minor stuff our husbands managed to stay ahead of by checking things out once in a while. As soon as I graduated, Rod and I realized we needed to trade cars. I had worn that old Oldsmobile completely out. If I remember correctly, we had to find a different car before it was time for me to go to Springfield to take my state board exams!

One day, about halfway through the year, I ran into a gal I had gone to school with who owned and operated a beauty shop in Pittsfield. I jokingly asked her if she had room for a second operator. She surprised me by saying, "no but we have been thinking about putting in another station. My shop is big enough to do that. If we do, will you come to work for me?" I told her I definitely would. That was a great feeling to know that I had a job waiting for me when I finished school.

We had to work pretty hard to get our classroom work done. On the days we were not busy in the shop they made us work on mannequins that had hair like a horse's tail! Imagine pin curling or finger waving hair like that! What a waste of time. There was a lot of nonsense that went on, but it was a good experience for me. At least I learned enough to walk confidently into the room with my model (my loving mother) on the day we took our state board exam and pass with flying colors. We were notified by mail that we passed but never were given our grade. That bugged me for a long time. Looking back, I wonder if they even bothered to give us one. I think we were judged largely on our appearance of self confidence and on our personal appearance. I was told by our instructor that it was a good idea to buy a new pair of shoes (white uniform shoes) and wear our best uniform.

The hard part of that year was dealing with all that was going on at home at night and getting my homework done. There was a lot of memorizing to do and my brain felt rusty. That was also the year that Vince was in third grade and had to learn his multiplication tables. After supper and dishes were done, we would go upstairs and work until everyone was out of patience. All of my kids were good students except Vince. He had a hard time and informed me one night "Mom, you know my memorize isn't very good!" However, after he got into fifth grade at Higbee School (which I was positive would be his total undoing) he improved and sailed the rest of the way through school getting average grades. Vince never did do the things I worried he would do but instead, always surprised me. Sometimes good...sometimes not. Of course, that was true for all of the kids. I would go downstairs and try to do my homework after using all my energy getting everyone else to do whatever they needed to do. Sometimes I would try to con Karma or Mitch into coaching me when I studied, but they hated that and most of the time I had to do without their help. When it was time to practice on someone's hair, I always made Vince be my model. His hair was naturally curly and easy to work with. Bless their hearts, all of them, it was a very hard year.

One Friday evening, shortly before graduation, our school had entered a float in a parade that was going on in Roodhouse. On our float we were just having a "class," so it was no big deal about costumes except for Miss Brenda, who was riding the float as our teacher. She needed a white uniform to wear. She normally made her own clothes and used pastel colors. I think she ended up making a white "uniform" out of a sheet.

The night of the parade, we had a really good time and Rod brought all of the kids to see the parade so they could see Mom riding a float. For some reason I can't imagine, I felt proud that night, of myself and my family.

Before we knew it, graduation was over. During the last week of school, Miss Pat always treated the graduating class to a luncheon at her home. It was there that she told a very touching story about almost losing her son to a tragic and bloody accident. She told about how the doctor gave them no hope and how hard she begged God to save her son. After several hours of begging, she surrendered her will to God's in the matter and within the hour, the doctor came and told them that the boy was going to be OK. That was her introduction to her testimony about how she was a Christian and how we should always surrender to God's will in our lives. It made a huge impression on me because I was a Christian but was not surrendered to God's will in my life. I wanted my way and didn't really trust

God with my life. There will be more on that subject later… much more.

To celebrate my graduation, my friend Janet and I (Janet helped me with my kids so I could go to school in the first place) decided we needed to go out and celebrate. Rod was reluctant because we didn't drink or dance and really couldn't afford to go anyway. However, I told him I was going and he could either go along or stay home. We went out to dinner, dancing, and had a few drinks (he went along of course), and that turned out to be the beginning of a chapter in this book about my life that I wish I didn't have to write.

Me - second row next to last one on the right

CHAPTER THIRTEEN
The Wasted Years

Some people think of the number thirteen as unlucky. Let me say that I think of Chapter Thirteen as unfortunate. The celebration party turned out to be a lot of fun. It also gave Satan just the stronghold he needed to make me throw caution to the wind. I felt a very strong compulsion to try to make up for the years of my youth that had been spent accepting adult responsibilities. 'Sewing my wild oats' a few years late, if you will. I do not intend to try to make excuses. My life was void of adults that I could talk to except my parents, and there is only so much you can talk to your parents about. We had church friends, of course, but had gotten away from church just a little because of the hectic schedule during the months I had been in school. Besides, you don't tell your church friends your deepest, darkest secrets and feelings, do you? It would be years later before I would learn that you should be able to tell your church friends anything. I had tried talking to pastors but they either told me to grow up or just said what they knew you wanted to hear. The group of friends that we acquired during this period of time felt like real friends to me. They wanted to know all about me and they wanted to tell me all about themselves. At first this seemed like just what I needed to make up for the void in my life...especially my marriage relationship. It would be a few years and a lot of broken hearts later before I would finally realize this couldn't be further from the truth.

To begin with, the circle of girlfriends grew from one or two to about six or seven. This was not a bad thing...at first. We had lots of fun talking about kids and housework, furniture, hairdos and makeup...you name it. But as we became closer and spent more time together our conversations started getting more and more personal. We began talking about our husbands, relationships with them, and the ultimate subject…sex. All of us were happy with some aspects of our lives and unhappy with other aspects. Well, duhhh!! That's life. The problem was, before long we were all convinced that we had the worst husbands in the world for a wide variety of reasons. Then we all began to sharpen our skills as men bashers. The more laughs we got from each other the nastier we got. It was great fun, after years of unmet needs and loneliness, it was great to have all these friends that understood what we were feeling and gave us permission to say anything we wanted about our husbands no matter how hateful. The more outrageous the bigger the laughs. Then a subtle thing started happening. Each one of us, without telling each other, began to feel like we had perfect reasons to get out of the marriage and try to find new lives for ourselves. We also believed all our friends had the right to do the same. Then we actually began to share with our husbands, beasts that they were, how awful all our friends' husbands were! This was a really big mistake. All of the husbands knew that all of the wives were unhappy! By this time we were spending lots of time together as couples out partying and dancing. Also, we all had boats, so we spent weekends together as families on the rivers and beaches. The husbands began thinking that they had the power to make these unhappy women feel better, and various things began being said and done that were out of line. Satan was in full control. I can't speak for any of the other wives, but I was disgusted by all men, especially the ones in our 'group'. After about three or four years of this nonsense, I got so tired of it I thought I was going to go crazy. I'm not trying to say I didn't enjoy the attention from the guys because I did, at first. It was the main thing missing in my marriage. But I knew it was horrible and hopeless, and if I could have traded husbands with someone it would not have been any of those guys in that group. I was still naive enough to think there was a man out there somewhere that I had not met yet that would be perfect for me.

    One night when I was walking home, it was late and very quiet and I had had too much to drink, I heard a voice in my heart that said, "OK Connie, it's time to grow up." Not one, but two of the husbands had been trying to talk to me and warn me that the other one was 'after' me. It made me sick! Even though I was "under the influence" I had enough sense to know that enough was enough. I not only wanted out of my marriage but out of the circle of friends as well. I wanted to crawl in a hole and die. The problem is you can't do that. I decided to try. It took a long time to get out of the marriage. I told Rod I wanted a divorce. I told the kids it was going to happen, and then I had to do practically everything for him to get him out of the house. I would learn that as painful as all that was for Rod and the kids, and for me because of the pain it caused us all, it was also very difficult to break the hold my friends had on me. They would not take no for an answer, nor would they accept my excuses. I didn't have the nerve to tell them that I was just as sick of the kind of relationship I had with them as I was of the relationship I had with my husband. Nothing would do but that I continue going out with them, even when I no longer had an escort. Looking back, I think some of them were subconsciously hoping I would stick around and take their husband off their hands! That way they would be free but would come out smelling like a rose. No, thanks!

One night while I was out with my 'friends', I met a man I had been briefly introduced to a year or so before and he took a very determined interest in me. He was good looking and I liked him, but the best part was, he was nobody's husband and I thought that would relieve me of all guilt. He knew all the right things to say, which I enjoyed, but I also saw him as a way to get out of the party circuit. He was not friends with anyone in our group and I saw that as a good thing. He would call me and talk to me, even come to my house and drink coffee and talk. I wouldn't go out with him because I wasn't divorced yet, but he started showing up everywhere I went and it wasn't long before I could no longer resist. I started divorce proceedings as soon as I could and then I told myself I was free to go with anyone I pleased. I also told my friends we didn't want to go out partying any more, which was true.

His name was Rudy. The more we saw each other the more we enjoyed each other. I found out after a few weeks that he was eight years younger than me, and I had a hard time with that. It was the least of his worries and as it turned out it was never a problem for us, but I never did really get used to the idea and didn't like to talk about it. We had so much in common that most of the time I didn't even think about the age difference. He was a workaholic and so was I. He could fix things and take care of things which was something I had never had anyone do before. He believed in taking care of things and keeping them in top shape. So did I. I told him not to even say the word "marriage" to me, but the day I got my divorce, he asked me to marry him. I said, "I don't want to talk about it for at least a year. I do believe that it must have been a year to the day that he asked me a second time to marry him. At first I was reluctant for several reasons. The main one was that he was not a Christian. I told myself, and Satan assured me I was right, that it didn't matter. I would win him to the Lord later. However, I never really talked to him about it.

Another reason I hesitated was because of the boys. I talked to them several times, but they assured me it was OK with them. They just wanted me to be happy. I know now that they knew it wouldn't do any good to tell me the truth about how they felt. By this time Karma was gone from home and married and didn't really care. She wanted me to be happy and it did impress her that Rudy would do so many things around the house for me and take care of my car. He even took care of the yard for me.

Rudy had been married before and had two little boys. We never got to see the youngest one, but the one that was three years old came to our house several times. Vince and Troy enjoyed him a lot and he enjoyed them too. That relationship was never meant to be because his mother couldn't stand the idea. She and Rudy couldn't even talk on the phone without getting into a fight and she just cut Rudy off from seeing him at all. He stopped paying child support (against my advice) to get even with her.

There was a time or two that I didn't like something Rudy said to one or all of the boys, but I told myself it was nothing to worry about. Life cannot be perfect. I do believe I must be the world's best self-deceiver. There were plenty of warnings that should have told me to back off. I wouldn't listen. At one point there was even another man who was interested in me who would probably have been a much wiser choice, but I was afraid to give it a chance. The thing is, I was once again in the process of making a life changing decision without asking or even wanting to think about what God wanted me to do. The people I talked to about it loved me, and they also knew me. They didn't want to tell me the truth about how they felt. I just kept telling myself everything would be OK. Looking back, I have a hard time believing I could make so many bad decisions. It was largely a control thing, I think. I wanted to be in control and have things my way. Selfishness.

Rudy made me feel like I was a very special person and he could not live without me. We had lots of fun together, working, shopping or just doing nothing. I felt like I understood him, even his bad moods. He had been in Vietnam and told me a few stories about what it was like for him over there. I knew that those experiences could sometimes affect a person's moods. I made up excuses for him. He also told me some stories about his childhood that helped me understand some of his ways and opinions about raising kids. I just kept on making excuses for him, to myself and others.

I also felt like he was the first man I had ever had a relationship with that understood my needs and what made me happy. I didn't spend nearly enough time considering my children and how it would work out for them. I told myself that I needed help raising the boys and he would help me. I also needed help taking care of the house, car, yard, etc. I knew he would jump right in and help with all that and he did. Last, but not least, I needed help financially. Rod was paying child support, but I was only working part time in my beauty shop. I wasn't coming close to making ends meet.

I had, several years earlier, borrowed the money and built on a room so I could have my own beauty shop. At first the money was good because I had built up a fair-sized business while working for Janet, and most of them followed me. At least one of my goals had been met and it was a decision I had never regretted. I enjoyed being home with the kids so I didn't have to worry about what they were doing. However, when Rod and I divorced, I was not making enough money to support my family even with the child support and soon found myself in pretty tough circumstances financially. Rudy was driving a truck and making big money when we met. A few months into the relationship he had changed jobs so he would be home nights and weekends to spend time with me. The money was not as good, but we didn't care. We just wanted to be a family.

I finally agreed to set a date for the wedding. It was June 27, 1975. We made our plans for a private wedding. Very private. Just Karen and Harold, Rudy and I, and the preacher. I left the boys home for a few days so we could go on a short honeymoon. I have to say, it was a wonderful trip. We went to the Ozarks but after about three days we were ready to go home and get busy living our life together.

The bliss was short lived. After we had been married two weeks he came home and told me he had lost his job! It was just because of his belligerance that this happened and I wondered what I had gotten myself into. I wondered that even more when I began helping him with his resume and discovered that he had actually had a different job every year since he had been out of high school! (Excluding the Army, of course.) I thought I had asked all the questions there were to ask before I married him, but this one never occurred to me. "How many jobs have you had since high school?" Well, we worked up the resume, which took a long time, and he hit the streets with it. I give him credit…he went out every day looking. Ended up with a temporary job putting up a machine shed for a farmer that took most of the summer. He would not apply for unemployment. It was beneath his dignity. But he hit the streets again in the fall and finally landed a pretty good job with International Harvester. The pay was better than his last job and there was good insurance. We were elated and I started to believe I had made the right decision after all.

Chapter Fourteen
Roller Coaster Ride

In August, before Rudy went to work at International Harvester and before the kids had to go back to school, Dad asked me one day if I thought Rudy would do the driving if he and Mom paid all expenses for a vacation. They wanted to take one last big vacation before they got too old. Dad said, "we would like to go to Florida and take the kids to Disney World." They wanted to be gone a full two weeks! None of us had a problem with that, so plans were made, suitcases packed, and we were off. Poor Karma had to stay behind and take care of our dog, Monte. My mother made the comment that we would be fortunate if we made it through this trip and were all still speaking to each other when we got home.

I had never been anywhere worth talking about since I had moved home from Colorado in 1958. It was now 1975. My kids had never been anywhere except the Ozarks a couple of times. We were excited and couldn't believe it when the time finally came that we were actually on the road. I was amazed at the sight of the big highways. All the traveling I had ever done was before the time of the four lane expressways. We decided that we would drive about 6 hours a day and always stop at least by 4:00 p.m. to get a room so we would have plenty of time to enjoy the swimming pools. Then we would go out to eat and get to bed early, ready to rise and shine the next day. I had never dreamed of having the opportunity for such an adventure.

Our goal was to leisurely make our way to the Atlantic Ocean and spend three days on the beach after we had been to Orlando and Disney World. Then when we were ready to make our way home, we would head north up the coastline so we could feast our eyes on the ocean as long as possible. Disney World was wonderful and an unforgettable experience, but for me, nothing would compare to the sight of the Atlantic coming into view for the first time, the sight of the sun coming up over that ocean, or the pleasure of walking into that cold saltwater. On our way down, we stopped to gaze upon the Gulf of Mexico and make our way through the sand crabs, which totally grossed me out, and wade in the warm Gulf water. On the way home we made our way through the Smokey Mountains of Tennessee and other wonderful places too numerous to mention.

It seemed to me that we had the best of everything in that trip. None of us will ever forget it and twenty plus years later we still talk about it once in a while. Even the few bad experiences we had gave us cause for much laughter for years to come. Mom's concern that we would hate each other by the time it was over did not come to pass. The boys were very well behaved and helpful with the work necessary for that kind of trip.

Mitch had just gotten his driver's license and Rudy actually encouraged him to help drive. Never a cross word was said by or to anyone or even about anyone that I know of. It is a wonderful memory that I will thank my dad for until the day I die.

My only regret is that Karma was not able to go with us. She said to me one day after the trip, "Mom, do you realize that everyone I loved was in that car going who-knows-where for two weeks?" That's when I realized a little how she felt when we left. I had that same feeling when Karen and Harold took off several summers with Mom and Dad for long vacations. I would imagine Karma's feelings were more intense than mine, though. The fact that she had never been anywhere and didn't dream she ever would didn't help either, I am sure.

When we finally did get home, it was good to be there. We had our memories to last the rest of our lives, but it was good to spread out and get away from each other for the first time in two weeks! We soon got back into the routine of everyday living, and it didn't take long to see that all was not well in "Utopia." It seemed that Rudy felt he had the right to tell me how to raise my kids and I couldn't have agreed less with some of his ideas. They were, for the most part, based on his own upbringing and his own desires.

What hurt me was that he made me feel like I didn't do anything right. Not just with the boys, but everything. He was sarcastic and critical and angry a lot of the time. How he managed to hide that from me before we were married, I will never know. I do remember noticing that he was somewhat defensive when we were dating and asked him about it. He admitted he was but had a way of making me think it was because his life before me had been unhappy and that I was just what he needed to make everything OK. It was many years and many tears later before I would finally learn that it was his job to make himself happy, not mine!

We had a lot of good times too. A lot of the time we were in a major redecorating or repair project on the house and we got along great. I guess it was because I trusted him to know how to do everything, which he did, and was more than happy to let him make all the decisions and tell me what I could do to help. I was always his "gofer". I appreciated his abilities and willingness so much that I praised him to death. I received very little praise from him for anything I ever did, and I worked like a dog just the same as he did anyway. I sewed my own clothes and shirts for him and the boys. I made curtains, tablecloths, pillow covers…you name it. We had two big gardens and I canned and froze everything from strawberries in spring to tomatoes in the fall. All of this while taking care of my family, a ten-room house, and working part time in my beauty shop (which Rudy was constantly telling me was not worth the money it took to pay the bills it created). He wanted me to "get out and get a real job." Kept telling me I had forgotten what it was like to get up and go to work every day! I had not forgotten. That was why I didn't want to do it! I got up at 6:00 a.m. every day and worked until 10:00 p.m. at night most of the time. I guess it was my pay he didn't like.

When we would get away for a shopping trip and supper out, mostly in Quincy, we always had a good time. He treated me more like a date than his wife on those occasions. We didn't do that very often and it was a treat for both of us. We enjoyed the same stores and restaurants and even the same kinds of food. I guess it was the diversion from everyday life that made it good. We could usually make it through the rest of the day and the evening enjoying each other after we would get back home. Sometimes we would spend a little money I felt we couldn't really afford, and I would worry about it. He would always reassure me about it. But, if I went to Walmart on my own and bought something for myself, he would make me feel guilty. He didn't do that if I bought something for the boys or him..just myself. I could never figure out what he wanted from me and sometimes I would tell him so. He didn't know what I was talking about.

As I continued to struggle with the relationship, I soon felt the desire to get back into church. It had probably been five years since I had gone to church regularly. One day I decided to approach Rudy with the idea of going with me. Bad idea! He told me to go right ahead and go, in fact he encouraged me. He always went to the Cardinal Inn on Sunday mornings for coffee and gossip, and I guess he figured I could go to church in his absence. I started working on the boys, preparing them for the idea that they were going to get up and go with me. Again, I struck out. I knew it was my own fault for falling away when they were the most vulnerable, but I was determined to fix it. I am sad to say that it was not to be. They gave me such a hard time, I gave up on them. It was easier to get up early, put a roast and all the trimmings in the oven, and get ready to go all by myself. I had trouble making myself go at first. Felt like an outcast. It was easier to fight my battle without fighting the boys too. I will never forget the sad and heavy feeling I would have every Sunday after church as I would walk by myself from the car to the house. Tears would actually be running down my face. Not once in a while, but every Sunday. It wouldn't be long before I would know the reason why.

A few months after I was back in church (long enough for me to lose the outcast feeling!) the church had a series of revival meetings. I vowed I would be there every night. I was. In fact, to my surprise, I found myself thinking about it during the day and I would get excited with the desire to go again that night. I remember being surprised at myself. In past years, when I went to revival meetings every night, it had been something I felt I had to do. This time it was different. God was about to finish the job he had started on me way back when I was walking home from that party one summer night. The time He told me it was time to grow up. Praise God for his patience! The evangelist was preaching a series of sermons on being "Filled with the Spirit." I wondered what that meant and how to go about it. It was getting close to the end of the week. One night the sermon turned into a mental dialogue between me and the speaker. It went like this "I wonder what you have to do to be filled with the Spirit?"

"All you have to do is say, "Please fill me with Your Spirit."

"Dear Lord, please fill me with Your Spirit!"

At that moment, something I could feel physically rushed into the very center of my being and I thought, "So, that's how it's done!" I left the building in wonder but didn't say a word to anyone. It was several weeks after that, I was cleaning house one day and thought to myself, "I am not the same person I used to be." I knew God had really done something in my heart and in my life. I wanted to tell people about it. Especially Rudy and the boys. The boys always ignored me, but Rudy always blew up at me. He "didn't need it, didn't want it, didn't want to hear any more about it!" I was never able to get him to go inside the church with me. There were a few times that I tried to talk to him again but the reaction was always the same. He had been "taken to church when he was a kid by Uncle Willie and Aunt Agnes and they were hypocrites!" He wanted to believe that when you are dead, you are dead and that's the end of it. I told him someday he would wish that was true.

When I would talk to the boys, I would remind them of

how they had been saved and baptized at the same time and ask them if that had meant anything to them. The only answers I got were, "church is boring and/or I don't want to go." I remembered so well when Troy had asked me what you had to do to be saved. I think he was about nine years old, and Vince would have been twelve. Troy and I talked about it and I explained as best I knew how. This happened shortly after Rudy and I were married and before the revival I talked about that really got me excited about being a Christian. I asked Troy if he wanted to go in my room with me and pray to ask Jesus into his heart. He said "yes," and we did just that. He felt better, he told me, and said he would go forward the following Sunday to make it public and to tell the church he wanted to be baptized. When invitation time came that Sunday morning, guess what? Vince beat Troy down the aisle! I didn't even know he was thinking about it. I asked him years later if he had heard Troy and I talking and he said he hadn't. He just knew he needed to be saved.

This is when I really let those boys down. I was going to church on a hit and miss basis and a few weeks after they were baptized, they started giving me a bad time again about going to church. As I said earlier, I didn't try hard enough to make them get up and go. If I had, I feel like maybe Vince's life would have turned out better. Troy has been fortunate enough to find a good wife and a good life, but Vince has not been so fortunate. Of course, I really can't take blame for Vince's misfortune. He is an adult and makes his own decisions. He has just simply made some bad decisions that made his life what it is today. After all, he is related to his mother!

Having said all that, after a time of off and on churchgoing on my part, I finally got serious about it. Then came the revival in which I really got excited about Jesus. I was happier than I had been in my entire life, and I didn't come home from church every Sunday crying anymore. I began praying for Rudy and the boys. By this time Mitch and Sherry were dating and were back in church. They got married in June of 1980 and then Karma and Karl got married on May 31, 1981, and they were in church too. I guess it was at this time in my life that I really felt God's love for me and my family and His unwillingness to give up on us. How I praise Him for that! I was confident he would bring Rudy to his knees, and Vince and Troy too.

It was not to be so for Rudy. At least not while he was a part of my life. The closer I got to God, the more I went to church and got involved, the more he seemed to resent it. His encouragement in the beginning turned into bitterness and more anger. I was told more times than one that "one of these days you are going to wake up and find me gone." I didn't believe he would leave me. We seemed to fight more and more and nothing was ever resolved or put to rest. It got so it was too hard to fight anymore. Then we found we didn't have anything to say to each other. He had never given up drinking completely, but it had never been a real problem. However, when we got to this point, it started being a problem. I was ashamed of him for sitting uptown in the worst hell hole in Pittsfield every Saturday afternoon and getting drunk. Then he began going out on Sunday afternoons. The next thing I knew he was going out at night and coming home so drunk he was throwing up. One night he actually slept on the bathroom floor. I couldn't talk to him at all. He didn't want to hear anything I had to say. One day he told me he was going to look for an apartment and move out. I still didn't believe he would do it. I knew he loved me in spite of all this. He was hurting and I had the answer, but he didn't want it. It made him mad. I believe he had found a woman he was interested in and decided he preferred her to me and my God and the church. I had found cigarette butts in the car ashtray with lipstick on them and when I asked him about it, he looked at me as if to say, "none of your business," and didn't even answer me.

He rented an apartment and moved out the following weekend. I wasn't really worried about it at first. He had done that before and then called me begging to come home by the end of a week. It didn't happen this time. After he had been gone about a week, Troy saw him out walking with another woman. I knew he would not be back, and I can't tell you how hurt and how angry I was. I thought I was going to die from the pain. It was physical sometimes. I remember leaving the church after Sunday school one Sunday because I was crying uncontrollably. My Pastor, David Church, ran me down and said, "Connie, I don't know what's wrong with you, but I have a good idea. Just remember that God loves you." I would remember and trust in those words more times than I can count. I still can't talk about them without coming to tears. I knew it was true and it comforted me.

Me, Rudy, Mitch, Vince, Mom, Troy

Chapter Fifteen

Pain and Gain

I went to work every day and did my job as usual. I had to bite my lip to keep from crying most of the time that I was not busy thinking about my work. It was awful. The thing is, it seemed to go on forever. Every day I would get up thinking I would feel better only to discover that I didn't. There seemed to be no less pain after several months had gone by. Finally, after about six months, I began to feel a little better. I was beginning to realize that I didn't cry quite as much. For all the fighting we had done and as hard to deal with as Rudy had been, I missed him but I was getting used to him being gone.

Then I heard that he and the other woman had gotten into a big fight (in public) and broke up. It made my day! If that wasn't enough, a prominent bachelor in town who I was waiting on at the bank one Saturday morning asked me for my phone number! I gave it to him, but I didn't think he would call me. He called that evening and asked me if I would like to go out to dinner with him. I accepted his invitation. We drove to a well-known restaurant and had a nice fish dinner. All I could talk about was Rudy. I was so nervous about being out with this man that I talked even more than usual. He finally reached out and put his hand on mine and said, "Relax, we are just having dinner, not making a lifetime commitment!" That made me laugh and put me at ease and we enjoyed the rest of the evening. He told me later that he was shocked at what good company I was. Talk about a boost to the old ego. Here I was, forty-seven years old, had been diagnosed with rheumatoid arthritis, and was getting divorced for the third time, and someone actually thought I was good company.

That relationship turned out perfect. Tom was gone on business all the time and only called me occasionally when he was home to talk on the phone. It was amazing to me that all he really wanted was someone to talk to. He told me things about his family and I felt he actually needed someone to listen to him. He was genuinely interested in what was going on in my life as well. When I told him my soon to be ex-husband had called me and was very upset that I had gone out with him, he thought it delightful. So did I. I told Rudy it wouldn't matter who I went out with he wouldn't be able to stand it. He admitted I was right.

I guess it would suffice to say here, that unless you have ever been single and close to fifty years old, you have no idea what kind of guys are out there. Looking back, I wonder why I didn't give up on it and keep my distance. I guess I was still hoping I would find Mr. Wonderful. I probably had dates with at least half a dozen men that made their intentions clear and I never went out with them a second time. One in particular comes to mind. It was a blind date, of all things! The girls at the bank thought it was fun listening to me make fun of all these guys. This particular man, whose name I can't remember, stepped up on my porch and I thought he was OK looking.

Maybe this would be interesting. We talked for a short while and then went to the Red Dome Inn for coffee. He kept telling me all about himself and what a warm and loving person he was. He told me a little about his ex-wife and then began asking me questions about my life. The first thing he wanted to know was, "are you a warm and loving person?" I began to get the picture. To make a long story short, I let him know I had no intentions of being "warm and loving" and after we sat there for two hours, I told him I wanted to go home. I was embarrassed that the waitress had come to our table three times to see if we were ready to order and he told her not quite yet! That night as I went over it in my mind, I decided the girls would want to know what this guy looked like. He had a bald head and big ears; wore dark rimmed glasses and had a big mustache...then it hit me. I had been out with Mr. Potato Head and he didn't even spring for dinner!

I had another friend who only wanted to talk on the phone. He had a longtime girlfriend but enjoyed other ladies' company as well. He only took me out once, for pizza, but he would call me often and we would talk for hours. It was fun. One night he called, my daughter and granddaughter were there, and we were making Christmas candy. I invited him to join us and he did. He enjoyed 'taste testing' for us and he enjoyed my granddaughter. Sometime later he got sick and learned he had cancer in his hip. The next thing I knew he was in the hospital dying. I felt bad about it because I had talked him into seeing a doctor. I figured he would end up with hip replacement surgery and be as good as new. It was much worse than that and I think he knew it would be. I was never interested in him romantically, but I missed him when he was gone. He had made me laugh.

Just when I thought I could care less about what Rudy was doing, (by this time he had moved to Kentucky and I was glad.) someone at work told me he was getting married! I couldn't believe how bad that hurt me. I was devastated. Lo and behold, just before he was to take his new woman (not his wife for a long time) to Kentucky to live with him, he called me one night. He said he just wanted to hear my voice. We talked for over an hour. I begged him not to do it. He said it was too late. I told him I still loved him. He said he loved me too and always would. I asked him what he thought he was doing. He said, "you don't understand." That was a major understatement! He would tell me he wished he had been a better husband with one breath and then ended up telling me he still thought it was all my fault the marriage didn't work. I told him I guessed we didn't have anything more to talk about and hung up. That was the last time I talked to him.

About this time, our church decided to have a very special study group entitled *Masterlife*. It would be a once-a-week meeting in someone's home with daily homework and lots of memorization. I couldn't wait to get started and volunteered my home for the meetings. It was all about discipleship and I was about to get serious about becoming a disciple. I had witnessed to every one of the men I have been talking about, but most were not the least bit interested. However, I was having a good time telling them how important God and the church were to me. Then when we got into the *Masterlife* study, I found out what it really means to be a disciple. I wrote an article about how much it had meant to me, both spiritually and emotionally, and sent it to the Illinois Baptist newspaper. To my surprise, they published it!

During this time one of the ladies coming to my house for the meetings was single, had never been married, and she and I started running around together. We went out to eat every Friday night and went shopping a lot on Saturdays. I didn't have much money, but we had a good time, and it was good for both of us. After *Masterlife* was over (and we had recuperated from all the hard work) we decided to go on a trip to Eureka Springs, Arkansas. We left early on a Saturday morning and got home on Wednesday evening. I spent money it took a year to pay off, but it was worth it.

We stayed in an old hotel that had a rich history, went to the town's quaint little Southern Baptist Church on Sunday and did a little sightseeing. On Monday we rode the trolley from in front of the hotel to the downtown shopping district, which was also quaint, for a day of shopping. On Tuesday we did some more sight-seeing and shopping and then visited the "Christ of the Ozarks" and topped it off with the famous Passion Play. We spent as much time at the hotel as we could just seeing the grounds, swimming, and we indulged ourselves one evening meal in their very-expensive dining room. Before we knew it, it was Wednesday morning…time to pack up and go home. This trip did a lot for me in more ways than one. I think that it taught me a woman can be complete without a man in her life. In fact, it may have helped me decide that I preferred it that way.

After we returned home, we got back into our normal routines and I became quite content with my life. By this time Vince and Lori were married and it was just Troy and me in that big old ten-room house. He took care of the upstairs and I took care of the downstairs. He took care of the yard and I took care of cooking, laundry, grocery shopping, etc. It was a good life for me, but Troy was lonely. He wanted to be married and have a family of his own. One night he came home in one of his "crazy" moods and told me he had met a girl. He was anxious to tell me all about her and I was happy for him except for the fact that he was my last child and I didn't like the idea of parting with him.

It was interesting to watch their relationship grow. Karissa was only 16 when they met. Troy was 18. At first, she was reluctant to "get serious" because she was so young and had barely dated anyone else. Troy hung in there for about a year and then Karissa decided he was the one for her. It seemed that at this point, Troy realized he had never dated anyone else and started thinking about looking around. Karissa hung in there for yet another year. Then they spent a year together. To quote Troy who said this in front of Karissa, "We are just staying together until one of us finds someone we like better." I always thought that was funny and also a sign that they really understood each other. Finally, they decided they loved each other and wanted to get married. They also knew they didn't want to wait long to start their family. I knew they had a special relationship, but I was reluctant to let go of Troy. I tried not to let him know how I felt but I don't think I fooled him for a moment.

They began making wedding plans and buying things for their "hope chest." I thought they were more mature than a lot of couples who had been married for several years. They had been together for four years by now which gave them time to work through things that surprise couples who get married and then find out they don't really "know" the person they married. It was fun watching them get ready for the big day. They spent a lot of time at my house and I enjoyed it. Sometimes they acted like I wasn't even there, but I still enjoyed it. I knew this situation was short lived, so I tried to prepare myself. It wasn't easy. I knew that soon they would have their own house and I had a hard time with the idea of being alone in that big old house.

I decided to sell that big old house. I put it on the market, but I really wasn't in a big hurry to sell. I had tried on my own before and had no luck, so this time I listed it with a realtor. I was pleasantly surprised to find out I was going to make a nice piece of money on it! When I told the kids I was going to sell it, I knew they wouldn't be happy about it. They would understand but wouldn't be happy. I felt I had no choice and went ahead with my plans. I knew that home is where Mom is. I don't think it bothered Karma as much as it did the boys, but we all had a hard time letting go. By this time, Mitch was in school in Colorado and it made him lose that "my home town" feeling. Vince was married and it made him wish he had the money to buy the house. Troy simply said, "This is the only house I have ever known."

Troy's wedding day finally came, June 5, 1988. All the kids were home, the big old house was full, and I was in a daze. I cooked and served the rehearsal dinner at my house because I couldn't afford to do anything else. I had done the same for Vince and Lori because they were married about seven months after Rudy left and it was all I could afford to do. It actually was quite a success and I felt it would be again. It was. The day of the wedding I remember walking out of that house to get in the car and I felt like I couldn't stand it. Troy had slept his last night under my roof. I made it through the day though, and had a good time doing it. When Troy came out to the altar for the ceremony, he looked at me and winked. It was the first time he had acknowledged the fact that he knew I was hurting. I lost it! But I got it together again and we had a good time that day. When we were all ready to leave after the reception, I told Troy and Karissa that I didn't want to horn in on their honeymoon, but I had all that left over food at my house and they were welcome to join us if they wanted to. She laughed and said, "Good 'cause I'm starving!"

At this point in my life, I had met a man who was a customer at our bank. His wife had died of cancer about a year before I happened to notice him one day. He seemed so sad and lonely. One Saturday, I got up the nerve to call him. (The first and last time in my life I ever did that!) He was gracious and we enjoyed a short visit, but he told me his wife had meant the world to him and he wasn't ready to think about someone else. He thanked me for calling and we hung up. Apparently, it gave him a boost to know someone was thinking about him, though, because the next time he came in the bank he came straight to my window and we had a nice little chat. He did that every time he came in after that. One day he told me he had sold his place and was going to move to Texas where his only daughter lived. I told him I was happy for him and wished him the best. He thanked me and expressed his feeling of appreciation for my friendliness. About six weeks later, during the Christmas season, I decided to look up his address and send him a Christmas card. To my surprise, he sent one right back and wrote a little note in it. We wrote to each other for six months and it was great fun. I looked forward to his letters and he appreciated mine. It absolutely took away all loneliness I had felt at times. After six months he wrote me to say he was coming home for a family reunion and said he would like to see me. I was elated.

He came in the bank on a Friday evening and asked me if I would like to go to dinner with him the next evening. I said I would love to and we made our arrangements. We went out the next evening and had a wonderful time talking about our families and our lives. He told me he had enjoyed it and asked if I would like to do it again. I said yes. He was to go to his reunion and come back through Pittsfield the following weekend. He said he would call me. He never did. Two weeks later, I got a letter of apology from him. He said he had visited his wife's grave when he went to the reunion, and he just couldn't come see me again. It made him feel guilty. He said he wished he enjoyed life like I did and regretted that he just couldn't see me anymore. I wrote back to tell him I understood and if I didn't hear back from him I would know he didn't want to write anymore. I never heard from him again and I missed his letters for a long time. I hope he ended up happy.

One Friday evening at work, I saw someone come in the front door of the bank I knew. I hadn't seen him for thirty years, but he hadn't changed a bit except his dark hair had turned snow white! It was "Ike". He came straight to my window and we talked several minutes. Long enough for him to ask me if I was married (which I found out later he already knew I wasn't) and tell me that he was getting a divorce. He said he would call me as soon as everything was all done. It couldn't have happened at a better time for me. When he called, we made plans to get together and we had a whirlwind good time all summer long. He took me places I had never thought of going. He loved good food and knew where to find it, sparing no expense. He was as jolly and as much fun as I remembered him from high school, and it was a healing thing for me. We really did enjoy each other, and he was soon asking me to marry him.

I knew I wasn't over Rudy yet and all he could do was talk about his ex-wife and how she drove him nuts. I knew deep down that I couldn't marry him, but didn't have the nerve to tell him. He finally planned a trip to Colorado so he could visit old friends and I could visit Mitch and Sherry. Usually, we had one evening a weekend and Sunday afternoon together, and then he would be off to his truck driving job. Looking back, I think that is probably why the relationship lasted as long as it did. I knew that this trip to Colorado would make or break us. We flew out there on Friday, stayed Saturday and Sunday, and flew home on Monday. By the time we got back to Pike County we both knew we never wanted to see each other again! I won't bore you with the details. Let's just say that I like to call all the shots and so does Ike. I will always be grateful for the big party he threw for my fiftieth birthday, though. I really didn't want to turn fifty! His family was so sweet and worked so hard to help him pull off a big surprise hog roast for me. It made turning fifty seem like a trivial thing because I really don't like surprises either! I think there were fifty people there and I only knew my family and half a dozen others! It was a nice thing for him to do and I appreciated it in spite of my shock. It was that day that I finally agreed to marry him, but I knew I wouldn't be able to do it. After the Colorado trip the relationship was history, and we were both glad to get out of it without either of us getting hurt.

Soon after the whirlwind romance, I had a buyer for the house. I went house hunting and found a cute little house just right for one person just two blocks from Troy and Karissa. I didn't do that on purpose, but we had a lot of laughs about it. If that wasn't enough, Troy and Karissa decided to go on a delayed honeymoon to Colorado and were kind enough to invite me. I went, of course, because Mitch and his family were there. It was over a year since I had been there, and I was more than ready to go again. Besides, I knew I would have a lot more fun this time and I did, even though I did get teased about going with Troy on his honeymoon.

Chapter Sixteen
The Winter of my Content

I adjusted quickly to my little house that was nice and clean, had new carpet and new furniture, and was so easy to take care of. I also adjusted to being alone much easier than I thought I would. When I had moved, Karissa was a huge help to me. We laughed and joked and had a good time together. I don't know what I would have done without her.

The boys did all the heavy lifting, but Karissa helped me put things away and get straightened up. It rained all that day, and Mom called to ask me if I was depressed about it. I told her I was just happy it wasn't hot because it was August. It was at this time that Karissa and I really got to know each other and our relationship became solid.

My life was busy but peaceful. I enjoyed working at First Bank as a teller and seeing people every day. I had lots of favorite customers and enjoyed my fellow workers as well. I tried to be a happy, fun-to-be-around person with a positive and encouraging attitude. I admit I had a lot of fun with my 'man bashing' jokes, and that is not right, but I just plain had fun at work almost every day. I really enjoyed going to work and I really enjoyed coming home to my little house.

By this time I was pretty heavy into doing things for Mom and Dad, but they were still doing things for me too. My favorite story concerning Dad's helpfulness is about toilet paper! I had a hard time making ends meet but it didn't worry me nearly as much as it did my dad. One day I made the mistake of telling him I had run out of toilet paper and had to use Kleenex for a week until I finally got paid. He was a 'buy lots of whatever is on sale' nut and every time they came to my house after I told him that, he brought me at least a four pack if not more! I had limited storage space and, unlike Dad, was not willing to stack it up in my spare bedroom. I finally had to make a joke of it and ask him to stop bringing me toilet paper. I had to promise him I would let him know if I ever got that broke again. I didn't tell him I was that broke most of the time. He couldn't have stood it.

I had flown to Colorado with Ike about a year before I sold the big house. But one day, when it was getting close to time for Mitch to graduate from college, Harold Dean told me they were going to Colorado for Mitch's graduation and invited me to go. I was elated and couldn't wait. I hate flying, but I love car trips and I love Colorado and I was so proud of Mitch I couldn't stand it. We made all our plans and were all looking forward to this wonderful trip. But just a couple of days before we left Mom got sick and ended up in the hospital in Quincy. I agonized over what to do but Karen told me I should go, and she would stay home and take Dad back and forth to see Mom. I felt so guilty I couldn't stand it.

Harold said we could do what we wanted but he was going to Mitch's graduation. Karma started the process of clearing herself so she could go in Karen's place. It's always hard for a wife and Mom to do that but she got the job done and we finally had things worked out.

Karma came to my house the night before we were to leave. Harold and Todd were to pick us up early that next morning. And I do mean early! It was still dark and it was pouring down rain. I was afraid Harold would decide not to leave that day, but he didn't. We loaded suitcases in the trunk of his car while rain was running down the backs of our necks and enjoyed it. We were off! I felt terrible about Karen staying home, but at the same time I knew she wouldn't have it any other way. It was a joy to have Karma with us. In a way I felt like it made up just a little for having to stay home when we all went to Florida. When we got out on the big highway, we made a game of writing down every state we saw car licenses from and ended up getting all but Alaska. I think we even saw one from Hawaii.

At last we got to Denver and Fitzsimmons Hospital where we were supposed to meet Mitch. We waited in the parking lot for over an hour. I knew it wasn't like Mitch to be late and began to worry. After a while we needed to go inside the hospital to find a restroom and there he sat in the lobby! That was a big laugh, and I was glad I went inside because Karma and Mitch had been born there. It was a very nostalgic moment for me, to say the least! Harold and Todd left to go visit Harold's sister and Karma and I headed for Colorado Springs with Mitch. Once again it was raining hard, but on the way the sun came out and a rainbow began dancing off the hood of the car. I felt like it was a visual blessing from God on our time together. I have a picture of that rainbow that I took through the windshield.

The graduation was wonderful and there will be more about it later. The only flaw was the weather. It was cloudy and cold, a rare thing for that time of year. Too soon we were headed for home. As is Harold Dean's custom, we left early in the morning and talked a mile a minute all the way back to Illinois. It just happened that the second day we were traveling was Karma's birthday. We made a routine stop at a rest area somewhere in Kansas and when Karma and I came back to the car we were in for a big surprise. After we had all retired to our rooms the night before, Harold and Todd sneaked out to a grocery store, bought a cake and a tube of decorator icing, and Harold decorated a birthday cake for Karma, candles and all! We had a little party right there at the rest area and added one more unforgettable memory to our list. The rest of the trip home was uneventful.

Carolyn and I continued our regular Friday night going out to eat routine and sometimes shopping on Saturday. By this time I was treasurer for the church and that kept me occupied several evenings a month. I enjoyed it and still do. My health was getting worse, and I didn't feel like going a lot of places. I was content to come home from work, fix a little supper, and sit in my chair in the living room watching the news about the war in Saudi Arabia while I ate. That little house was extremely easy to take care of and Troy took care of my yard for me. The only time I didn't like the house being so small was when some of the kids came home for a visit. It was crowded and they didn't feel comfortable. That's when we really missed the big house! It was especially inconvenient when we had Thanksgiving and Christmas celebrations. However, there are a couple of special memories we made in that house.

The bank was having a promotion which, among other things, offered people family photographs at a very special price. The first thing I thought of was, how nice it would be to have a nice photograph of me and my four grown children. I immediately dismissed the idea, believing it to be an impossibility. Then it dawned on me that it was the time of year Mitch and his family usually came for a visit. I talked to him first and he said he thought he could arrange it. Then I talked to Karma and she said she would make it work. To my amazement, we pulled it off. Don't think I don't love my in-laws and grandkids, but it was a nostalgic and proud day of my life when I walked out of my house and got into an automobile to go somewhere with my four children by myself. The pictures turned out wonderful and if I had a fire and could save only one thing, I think it would be those pictures.

I loved my church and the Pastor and his family. They had been so good to me when I went through the divorce. We became even closer after I had opened my big house to the *Masterlife* program. One day someone told me the Churches were leaving. I was not surprised but I was also not happy. However, I understood. The church had grown bigger than it had ever been and it became necessary to do something about a new building.

Nothing like a building program to stir up trouble and bring out the worst in people. Especially if the church is already troubled. David and Beverly Church saw the handwriting on the wall and announced their resignation. They left before I sold the big house and a new pastor was hired. That poor man didn't have a chance. Ultimately, he was forced to leave, and the church had gone so far downhill that there was no money to pay him for professional reimbursements he was entitled to. Since I was treasurer, he came to my house one day and we made an agreement for me to pay him so much a month until the debt was paid. He was very good about it. I asked him if he was leaving with a bitter taste in his mouth and he said no. "I have learned some valuable lessons while I have been here that

I am sure was in God's plan for my life." Eventually, several families left the church.

We ended up with a beautiful new sanctuary that was basically constructed by the Carpenters for Christ. They are a group of volunteers based in Talladuga, Alabama who build a new building every summer for a church in need. They were here for a week and we held services in our new sanctuary on Sunday in the middle of that week. There wasn't even a roof over the entire building yet, but it was a thrilling experience. I will never forget it. The choir that Sunday was the volunteers themselves. Some of the men from our church have gone every summer since then to help the Carpenters. The building was actually going on the same week of Troy's wedding when I was still in the big house. I had a busy time trying to get ready for that wedding and run back and forth to the church three or four times a day to take pictures. It was going up so fast you had to go that often to get an accurate portrayal of what was going on. In retrospect, everything about this difficult time in the life of our church happened according to God's will and in His timing which is always perfect. We are always in a hurry and want answers right now, but God knows what He is doing in every aspect of our lives and the life of a church.

After Pastor Yeager left, we had an interim pastor for over a year. He was a wonderful man who I respected and appreciated greatly. We were fortunate to have him, but it is always an undesirable thing to be without a pastor. By the time he left, a lot of the bad feelings had died down, but there were some people who would never forget some of the things that were said and done. I hold no grudges personally, but I will never forget the pain it caused everyone to see a loving church turned into a battleground. I vow never to go through that again. Looking back, I see that period of time as a chance given to us by God to do some healing before a new pastor came on the scene.

At last the word came that our pulpit committee was ready to call someone to preach for us and then the church would vote to hire him if it so desired. He was a young man, would be the youngest pastor we had ever had, and I was excited at the prospect. He was pastor of a small church in Bluffs and we loved him immediately. He was called and he accepted. That has been over eight years ago and he is still with us, still has a vision, and is patiently trying to get the entire church to have a vision as well. The church has exploded to an average attendance of one hundred forty. We have seen a lot of changes!

About the same time Eugene Guthrie became our pastor, I rekindled an old relationship with a man I had known when I was in high school. I had grown content to be by myself, realized that I could support myself, and wasn't sure I would ever want another man. However, I knew this man was a really good man and he had been left alone against his will. I had worked for his wife in her beauty shop years ago and was curious as to what happened to the long-term relationship he had had after his divorce years ago. I spoke to him one day as I was driving by his house and he motioned me to pull over. He was still very much in pain and was more than willing to tell me everything about it. I sat there listening to him until I felt like I needed to get out of the road and then invited him to my house "sometime" for coffee and conversation. He seemed in so much pain I didn't think he would ever do it. I really felt sorry for him, but I was not surprised at the way he had been treated. His name is Kenny Leahr.

Karma and Karl were going on a trip to Silver Dollar City, taking their nice big camper, and they had invited me to go along. I was looking forward to a nice week-long trip away from work, home, all the routine things of life. We were supposed to leave the next weekend after I had talked to Kenny on Sunday afternoon. That Sunday evening he called me and then came down. We talked for several hours. He was in a lot of pain but talking is great therapy and I felt like it did him some good to tell me about it. When he left, he told me he appreciated my hospitality and might call again. He assured me, however, that he was not looking for another woman or a wife. I didn't believe him. I didn't hear from him until the following Friday night and I had started believing him by then!

It was rather late when he called. He had been mowing the South Cemetery, but he asked if it was too late to get together, and I told him it wasn't. We had another good visit and when he was getting ready to leave I told him I was going to be gone for a week with my daughter and her family. I told him all about our plans for the trip and that I would be home on Memorial Day Weekend. He acted like he wished I wouldn't leave just then but he just gave me a little kiss and left.

The time came to leave, and I was excited. It was a fun trip and a treat to get to go somewhere I had never been. I had never camped either. Maybe it was not a good thing that my first camping trip was with kids! I love my grandkids to death, but we had a few problems. Livi was in a bad mood most of the time. Karissa was loud and every night they fought over who was going to sleep where. Devon never stopped talking, asking questions! I would tell him to stop talking and he would just laugh. One night I went to take a shower at the bath house and the thought came to me that I could sleep there! It would be more quiet! The good far outweighed the bad though, and Karma planned every day to be full and action packed. Her philosophy is, "if I am going on vacation, I want to get all I can out of every minute." She did. At one point, Karl and I were resting on a bench listening to live music while Karma was off on a water ride or something just as busy with the kids. Silver Dollar City was beautiful, and I did lots better than I thought I would when it came to walking up and down those hills. I enjoyed it a lot. We also saw a Passion Play that was far more elaborate than the one in Eureka Springs but I really didn't enjoy it any more (or less) because I knew what to expect. By the time we headed home, I was getting homesick. I had thought of Kenny a lot, even sent him a postcard, and when I would think of him, I got this warm, cared-about feeling. I was looking forward to pursuing the relationship. Livi said, "This isn't fair! I am supposed to have a boyfriend, not you, Mamaw!" But she laughingly dubbed him "the Kenmeister."

Karma's Birthday Cake

There is a Rainbow

Chapter Seventeen

One More Time

We arrived in Pittsfield on Monday of that Labor Day Weekend. We had finished unloading my things and were taking a break when I saw Kenny's old yellow car drive by the house. It made me think he had been watching for me to get home. We went outside to sit so that if he came by again Karma could meet him. He did drive by again and I went to the car to invite him to join us. He said he would wait until the kids were gone.

That evening he came down and told me he thought the week would never end. He thanked me for the postcard and told me he was already thinking about me more than he should. I told him I thought about him a lot too and we definitely decided to pursue the relationship and see what happened. When I had dated Kenny when he was young, I remembered him as very quiet and actually rather boring. I was surprised to learn that he was quite the talker.

We spent all our time talking about our past relationships, our children and my grandchildren (he didn't have any grandchildren), and our general thoughts and opinions about life. I was not long in bringing up the subject of Christianity. I knew him to be a totally good person but was reasonably sure he was not a Christian. That would not do. Any time I spent time with a man, even on the phone, I quickly let him know where I stood with God and the church. That is probably one reason I went out with most of them only one time. Kenny was very open to everything I had to say and the main thing I remember him saying in response to some of my many comments was, "I didn't know that." Sometimes he asked questions or repeated what I said, making sure he had understood me correctly. One night I remember telling him that he acted more like a Christian than some Christians I knew. I had made that observation about him and thought he needed to hear it. I told him I didn't think becoming a Christian would change his lifestyle that much. It wasn't long before he expressed the desire to talk to Eugene about making that commitment.

We weren't far into the relationship before he started talking about marriage. I worried that he would make his decision too soon after his previous relationship. I knew I had done that in the past and it had turned out badly. I also worried that he would make a "head" decision instead of a "heart" decision about Jesus because he knew I would not marry him if he was not a Christian. After Eugene talked to him and prayed with him, he seemed convinced that Kenny was sincere. Kenny started coming to church with me and within a few weeks, went forward to declare his commitment to Christ and to be baptized and become a member of Calvary Baptist Church. It was a memorable day.

Kenny's spiritual condition was not the only hurdle we had to get over before I was willing to get married again. I was gun shy, and I couldn't understand how he could possibly not be! I kept telling him he needed time to heal but he would not be convinced. He was certain he knew what he was doing. I even told him that I know I am not an easy person to live with. That I wasn't sure I wanted to get married again. That I had a large family, and he surely didn't want to get into that again. (He had only one son who was unmarried at the time.) That I was not in good health and it was going to get worse. I even told him that I had a bad attitude about men, and I couldn't promise him it wouldn't be a factor in our future relationship. He would not be deterred.

I finally agreed to marry him. Then he wanted me to set a date. I had a problem with it. At one point I almost backed out, but I couldn't do it because I didn't want to disappoint him. He sensed my dilemma and fervently asked me not to back out on him. In some strange way, I took comfort in the fact that he was capable of sensing my feelings. I had never known a man before who could do that or if they could they sure didn't let me know it. I didn't back out but there have been lots of times I have wondered if I should have done so for Kenny's sake. I knew my kids had misgivings about it, not because they didn't like Kenny but because they know me. They were just as sure as I was that he didn't 'know' me, and they were afraid we would both be unhappy. They didn't want to see me unhappy ever again.

Well, life is hard either way you go. I heard a preacher say once that people who were not married wished they were and people who were married wished they were not! I think he was right! At any rate, I decided to do it and we set the date for October 19, 1991. We knew we needed a much bigger house so we began looking and settled for a house I had always liked that would be just right for our lifestyle and our family when they visited us. I sold my little house to Carolyn, who had always liked it, and we got on with the business of our life together. We got all moved into the house, had a family wedding at the church and a family reception at the house. It was a hectic week and a fun day that was enjoyed by all. My mom and dad were so glad to know that I had someone to take care of me (Though I suspect they knew he had his work cut out for him!) They always worried about me being alone.

As is always the case, it was not long before bad things started happening. Kenny got word that the garage where he worked was going to be sold and he didn't know about his job security. He also got word there was a possibility of a job opening with Pike County Housing which he wanted desperately. I had a bad hip, and I knew I was not going to be able to work much longer. The bad thing about that was I had our health insurance at the bank. I know Kenny worried a lot about it all, but God took care of everything. Kenny got the job he wanted, and I was able to quit work. I got on disability and he got me on his insurance with Pike County Housing. The financial transition was uneventful and six months after he got his new job, I was able to have hip surgery. By this time we had been married about three years. We were also well into the normal struggles of adjusting to a new marriage, which, by the way, is harder when you are older and set in your ways. Poor Kenny found out that I wasn't kidding when I told him I am not an easy person!

Kenny believes in taking his time, I am always in a hurry. Kenny likes to stay up late and sleep late. I like to go to bed early and get up at a decent time. Kenny doesn't like to go anywhere. I like to go places once in a while. Kenny likes the back roads. I like the expressways. Kenny likes beef, I like chicken. Kenny likes to eat supper late. I like to eat early and get the mess cleaned up. Kenny likes to help me with my work, but he doesn't want me to help him with his work. Kenny would never give anyone an unkind word. I find lots of humor in being sarcastic. Kenny would walk around the edge of town to avoid confrontation. I enjoy a good fight once in a while, within reason, of course!

Kenny's ways of doing things are totally different than mine. Sometimes we both think the other one is strange. I think this paragraph will suffice to give an idea what we were up against (and still are) in adjusting to our life together. I know and so does he that none of these differences and all the differences I have not mentioned are not really important. They just seem like it sometimes!

Besides my health getting worse, Mom and Dad were going downhill fast. And Kenny's Aunt Grace was in and out of a nursing home, once before we were married and twice after we were married, before she died at the age of ninety. Kenny also has a brother, Roger, who was in a nursing home when we got married. He got better and we moved him to an apartment in Rushville. Kenny was very pessimistic about it, but Roger has done fine. That was over five years ago. Karen and I kept Mom and Dad at home as long as we could but when it got to the point that someone had to be there every day to do things for them, we began to despair. Then Dad had his second stroke, and the situation became impossible. There was no choice but to put them both at Pittsfield Healthcare Center.

Dad only lived two and one half months there. He got pneumonia and after a week in the hospital he died on September 9, 1996. He was almost eighty-four years old. Mom is eighty-one and still living there.

I will be sixty-two years old in one month and my health continues to worsen. I had foot surgery this past summer and can walk better as a result, but my feet hurt most of the time. I have to take so much medicine it makes me want to rebel. Kenny, on the other hand, prefers to think of himself as being in perfect health. He won't even take Tylenol unless he is in really bad pain. He knows he has high blood pressure but won't do anything about it. I think he just doesn't want to know if there is anything wrong and figures he will live until he dies. He was sixty-five years old seven months ago and is still working full time. You know what, he is right, and he will probably outlive me! I thank God that Kenny doesn't mind taking care of me. God knew I was going to need him whether I liked it or not, so he put him in my life. It's interesting how God takes care of us in spite of our stubbornness.

One day I was on the back porch shaking rugs and noticed a little house on the next street over that was being remodeled from the ground up. It occurred to me that it would literally be a new house when it was done. It was also smaller than the one we had, and I was getting so I had a hard time keeping up with the housework. Our house was a modular home and pretty to look at, open and light, very convenient. But it needed lots of work done and would always need something. I decided we would be ahead to get rid of it while the getting was good. I loved the idea of a 'new' house with no upkeep required and less space to keep clean. I started working on Kenny to win him over to my idea. It took some doing because he doesn't like change, but I finally got him to at least go see the house and talk to the owner who also is doing the work. The house was too small for Kenny's taste but the big problem for him was buying a house when we already owned one. To me, that is no big deal, but it worried Kenny until the day we sold the old house. One and one half years and two renters later, we sold the old house and made money on it! A word of advice here, stay out of the renting business! The first couple we rented to paid one months' rent and a deposit but we never saw any more money and they lived there almost five months. If that wasn't enough, she was paranoid and wouldn't let the realtor show the house. The second couple paid their rent, but they also had a problem with realtors. They finally moved out rather than worry about the realtors or having to worry about moving if we sold the house.

We have been in our new house over two years now and are quite happy with it. The only time it is too small is when kids and their families come for an extended stay. Of course, it is very snug when we have Thanksgiving and Christmas family get-togethers and squeeze twenty-five-plus people in here, but we have a good time anyway. I know we will be here until we die because Kenny told me when we were moving in that the next time he moved it would be two blocks west (Pittsfield West Cemetery.)

I say we will live here until we die. I hope that is true. I never thought I would see the day my parents were in a nursing home and neither did they. I have learned a lot about nursing homes since Mom has been there that I didn't want to know! We are fortunate to have her in a good one (as good as they get) but I am convinced that she gets good care because they know Karen will be there every day and I spend two afternoons a week there. Karen and I have friends that work there and friends we have made since Mom has been there. I am sure that helps. It doesn't matter how long someone lives there or whether they are in their right mind, they never stop wanting to go home or talking about going home. Sad and ugly things happen every day that Mom has to put up with. Worse than that, sometimes she is the cause of a problem like when she throws up at the dinner table or falls and scares them to death. Life is hard and it does not get easier.

In spite of all this gloom and doom, I want to say that I have enjoyed my life and I see it as a good one. God has loved me in spite of myself! Every decade has been better than the last in some way. Every decade has also been hard in some way. We have to choose whether we want to be happy or depressed. It is just as easy to be a happy person as it is to be unhappy. I took the time occasionally to be thankful for my youth when I was young. Now I thank God I don't have to go to work anymore and have all the difficult times behind me. I try to think about the positive things in my life and not be afraid of what might happen to me in the future. I know who holds the future and worrying will not change anything.

This is our second full summer in our little house and Kenny has finally got the yard all fixed up the way he wants it. He has planted trees and shrubs and lots of flowers. The landscaping looks lovely from the street. People are still commenting on this house and the improvement it has made in the neighborhood. I am quite proud of the inside and how pretty and homey it looks. I feel like we have done a good job on it and have had a good time doing it.

Chapter Eighteen

Grown Children

I could write a book about each one of my children, but I will leave that to them. I am writing my life story as I see it and they may want to write their own story someday! My heart is so full of love and gratitude for them that I have to write a chapter about the four of them however, and I will begin with the firstborn.

Karma Gene Sanderson was a sweet and loving little girl. She was beautiful and intelligent as well. I never had to worry about her getting her homework done or getting in trouble at school. When she was about eleven years old she began to show signs of an independent nature. Go figure! I blamed it on puberty, which was part of it I am sure, but having two little brothers who annoyed her to death and a brother less than one year younger with whom she was beginning to fight a lot didn't help matters. Then came the high school years and the boys. I have already told you how she helped me with my responsibilities when she was very young. Now I want to tell you how it paid off when she grew up. We got through the difficult years, but it wasn't easy. She was determined to leave home the night she graduated from high school, and she did. She had met a guy named Gary who wooed her with his guitar and love songs (not the first, by the way) and was convinced he was the one for her. They went to Springfield and were married three weeks later at the courthouse! I knew nothing about it until it was done. I made the decision to love Gary because I didn't want to lose Karma forever. It wasn't hard to love Gary…he liked me, and he could come to my house and be who he wanted to be. I tried to just let go and let them live their lives. Karma and I became friends for life.

After about a year and one half, Karma told me she was pregnant. For reasons I can't explain, I wasn't as happy about it as she wanted me to be. However, when that baby was born you would never know I didn't want to be a Grandma! Karma called me herself right after delivery and told me she had a little girl and had named her Olivia Anne. Within the hour, Mom and I were on our way to Memorial hospital in Springfield to see my first grandchild (we wanted to see Karma too, of course). I knew when I saw the beautiful baby with the pink bow in her hair that she was "ours."

Within two years Karma's marriage came apart and she found herself alone with a small child. She had a really rough life for about four years. At that time in my life I was still struggling financially and was unable to help her. She assured me that she loved Livi so much it scared her, and she was happy in spite of her circumstances. After a time she met a man named Karl Dunham who had two daughters and they eventually married. His girls' names are Diana and Karla. Karma and Karl lost their first baby girl at about six months into the pregnancy, and it was very hard for them. Karma named her Kara Michelle (Michelle after Mitchell). It wasn't long until Karma became pregnant again and this time everything went well. They named her Karissa Elizabeth. When Karissa was three years old Karma and Karl adopted a physically and mentally challenged three-year-old boy named Devon Michael who was wanted by no one until they decided they wanted him. He had spent his entire life in the hospital.

Karma helped Karl raise his girls, Karl helped Karma raise her daughter and together they have almost got 'their' kids raised. I have watched all of this and thought over and over how much better Karma has been than I was as a wife and mother. I love my kids dearly, but I don't think I could ever have raised my own kids and three that weren't mine!

The thing I admire most, and I admire lots of things about Karma, is her steadfast determination to follow God's will and seek His wisdom in all things. Unlike me, she has never wavered from His ways and has gone through some really bad things determined not to let Satan "get" her. She has maintained a happy and positive outlook on life no matter how difficult her circumstances. She keeps her physical body in good shape the same as she does her spiritual life. I know that there have been times that her commitment to God is the only thing that has kept her going in the right direction, both physically and emotionally.

Karma has always treated me like I am one of the most important people in her world. I have never gone to her house that she and Karl both didn't make me feel like they were really glad I was there. I thank her for it, and I know she will never have any regrets regarding me. She is my one and only, absolutely beautiful in every way, daughter.

Mitch was always a good little boy, but he managed to get into some trouble as all little boys will do. As he grew older, some of the trouble he got into was worse than I would ever have believed. I was always a sucker for Mitch's explanations and believed everything he told me. The funny thing about that is I made fun of other parents whose kids had pulled the wool over their eyes! I didn't find out about most of this trouble until it was entirely too late to do anything but be shocked and breathe a sigh of relief that I hadn't known before and nothing bad had happened to him.

For some reason I could never figure out, all of Mitch's friends managed to get good jobs when they got out of school and Mitch didn't. I knew, of course, that Mitch was smarter than all of them and would probably be a better employee too. However, he never got a job that paid more than minimum wage.

Mitch was shy with girls and never dated much. One day after he was out of school and working but still living at home, he told me he had met someone. Her name was Sherry. They made a commitment to one another within a year and within another year they were married. Mitch and Sherry got back into church before they were married, but they didn't get really serious about it until after they were married. Mitch would sit in the rock quarry where he worked for Callendar Construction and read and memorize scripture every spare minute he had. It kept his life from being boring, and God kept him in that 'going nowhere' job for a reason. After Mitch and Sherry had been married two years or so, they had their first daughter, Kirra Dawn Sanderson, and we were all thrilled to death. She had thick, long, black hair and was beautiful, to say the least. Sherry was so happy she couldn't stand it. To be a mom was her dream. Two years later they had precious Cacey Leigh and all was well. By this time Mitch was feeling God's call to the ministry. Thus the reason for time to read and memorize scripture was revealed. He knew that soon he would pack up the family and go to Colorado Springs to bible college. (That in itself is a book!) It was beginning to become clear why Mitch never could get a "good" job. He was going to end up working for the Ultimate Boss.

The four years in Colorado Springs were a nightmare for them in more ways than one, but Mitch kept the faith, worked like a dog, maintained a positive attitude most of the time and accomplished his mission. The first time I went to visit them, (my friends at work had taken up a collection for the plane ticket) I was scared to death of flying but had a wonderful time while I was there. I was there over a weekend and Mitch and I went to Denver for one whole day to visit all the apartment sites where Ralph and I had lived as well as Fitzsimmons Hospital where Mitch and Karma were born. I cried a lot that day, but it was another one of the most memorable days of my life. On the days Mitch was gone to work and school, Sherry and I would talk for hours on end and enjoy the kids together. Mitch and Sherry would stay up late at night with me and visit. This was when I found out about most of the previously mentioned "trouble" Mitch had gotten into in his young and foolish days. Now he was in bible college! When Mitch graduated it was a flurry of activity and a dream come true. Without a doubt one of the proudest days of my life. It still thrills me when I think about it. Some of the ceremonies were held outside in my beloved mountains and though the weather was threatening, I wouldn't change a thing except the fact that I forgot to take a slip with me and had to wear my "Colorado' tee-shirt under my dress to help keep me warm. Mitch told me I looked tacky because you could see the blue lettering through the dress and the tee-Shirt sleeves were longer than the dress sleeves! Thankfully, I had a jacket to wear.

After Mitch graduated, they moved straight to Marengo, IA. This was four or five hours away compared to eighteen. Nice improvement. He and Sherry have been in the ministry now for almost ten years, not including Colorado, and they are still in love with Jesus and enjoying their work. Just before they left Colorado, their son was born. Kristopher Aaron Sanderson is now nine years old and he is a delightful little grandson. I regret not having more time with Mitch's children. It has been hard for me to get to really know them because of the distance. But I have never had to worry about them being raised in a good and loving home. They have been in Britt, IA for the past six years.

Mitch and I have always been friends and I am really proud to say that. He has reason to be ashamed of me in some ways, but I know he loves me and respects me in spite of my mistakes. He has told me several times that watching me go through my struggles helped him keep his eyes on God and not give up. If I had to suffer because of my own pride, I am grateful for the knowledge that my kids (I believe Karma was helped by it too) could profit by my mistakes. Mitch's family makes a good team for God!

Vince was a busy little boy. He walked early, talked early and caused my nerves to have a bit of a relapse! It wasn't that he was bad, just busy. It seemed like I had to do everything twice because he always wanted to "help" me. I would let him help and then fix it later when he wasn't looking. He was very strong and could do anything from removing door knobs with a screwdriver to getting the very heavy top off a cistern and throwing everything in sight into eight feet of water!

God watches over little boys. I am convinced of that. He was also sick a lot. Just a few weeks after he was born, he had a close call with what the doctor said could have been a case of SIDS. It happened again the next winter when he was just over a year old, but it was not as severe. He had hernia surgery twice, various injuries requiring stitches, bad bike wrecks and one time even had a fishhook stuck through his eyelid. Rod told me to call the doctor and then rushed him to the ER. Dr. Bunting said, "Lets hurry up and get this taken care of before Mom gets here!"

Vince was always looking out for somebody, especially Troy, Jerrilynn and Todd. He could never stand to see someone being a bully. I find that interesting because he would put up with anything to avoid a fight, but he would fight for anyone he saw being mistreated. He is like that to this day. If there was such a thing as Tender Heart of the Year award, Vince would get it. We have a precious picture somewhere in the family archives of Vince spoon feeding Jerri when she was two and he was three. It is so typical of him. Vince thinks everyone is good to a fault. That wonderful trait has gotten him into trouble his whole life. I have never been able to force my suspicious nature on him because he is so much like his dad. He doesn't want to believe anything bad about anyone.

When Vince and Lori had been married about three years, she started wanting to have a baby. Vince wasn't ready but he finally gave in and by the time they had been married four years they had a daughter they named Leslie Michelle. Lori came down with diabetes during the pregnancy and it returned after the baby was born. Lori didn't feel well and was unable to keep up with the household chores while she was pregnant. Vince had always been good to help. In no time at all he was doing everything including taking care of Leslie. Eventually she and Vince were in the tavern every day. They developed habits that are very destructive and life changing. The marriage ended in divorce after fourteen years.

It is a heart wrenching thing. Leslie is a good girl, sweet and helpful. She can also be tough, and I wonder how well I really know her. She tries to be what she is expected to be according to who she is with. How confusing that must be to her. She is actually just growing up on her own. She is not sure how she is supposed to behave sometimes. What do you do when your child has a problem like that, and you can't do much to help? The whole family would like to help but our hands are tied.

The one thing we can do is pray for Vince and Leslie and we do it every day. They are not in church, and it breaks my heart. I know from experience that you can only get help and answers that are true from God. I wish Vince would give Him a chance. I pray and trust that he will someday. I hope it won't be too late for Leslie if and when he does. By his own admission, Vince needs a good woman to help him with his life. That is true, but what I want him to realize is that he needs Jesus first and Jesus will take care of sending him a good woman!

Vince is good-hearted to a fault and in a way that makes me proud of him. He would never be unkind or abusive. He works every day and has all his life. He does the best he can, but he has never given himself a chance. He would give you the shirt off his back and is always taking in "strays" but it seems like he just gets kicked in the teeth for his trouble. All we can do is continue to pray for him and Leslie and do what we can to help. I know Vince considers me his friend because he always calls to talk to me when something good happens to him or when something bad happens to him. He is not one to talk much, but when he is happy or sad, he needs to share with me.

I love it when my kids need me, even when I can't help.

I can't imagine life without Troy. He is as opposite from Vince as he can be. He was never a kid, always the little man. He gave me a little grief when he was growing up, but very little. Unlike Mitch, I think if there were things in his past that would shock me, he would keep it to himself instead of having fun shocking me! But don't get me wrong, Troy has plenty of good-natured fun at my expense. He can dish it out and he can take it. A kid after my own heart. We have a special bond that I hope doesn't bother the other kids. It is largely because I had more one-on-one time with Troy and in the end, he got stuck with taking care of me until he finally got married. Even after he got married, actually, because he had to do a lot for me until I married Kenny. I wonder if he gave me a big "thumbs up" behind my back when I told him we were getting married.

One night Troy came home from his usual night out, landed with a big flop (as big as he could possibly make it) on my bed, and announced that he had met a girl. My enthusiastic reply was, "I suppose her birthday is in May" (Karma, Sherry and Lori all had May birthdays). "Nope, it's in September, same as yours. Guess what her name is…Karissa!" Then followed my usual twenty questions about who she is, who is her dad, what does he do for a living, how old is she, etc. The exact same thing my dad did to me when I was dating that drove me nuts. I knew Troy really was ready for a relationship and I wanted him to find the one he wanted but I also did not want to give him up. At the same time, I was happy for him I also had a rush of panic go through me. Not just because I didn't want to give him up, but because I didn't want him to find out what real life is all about. I had that same feeling big time years later when Livi got married.

Karissa was a very quiet girl, and for a long time I thought she hated me. Just what I needed, a daughter-in-law who hated me and would probably live right here in the same town with me her whole life! Well, she is going to live here her whole life, but she doesn't hate me, and she is not quiet! We have a good time together. She just needed time to get used to me, imagine that. Sherry wasn't shy with me, and Lori certainly wasn't, so I didn't know how to deal with her shyness.

A short six months after they were married, Troy and Karissa were ready to have a baby. To their bitter disappointment, it took three years to get pregnant. The day came, however, when Troy called me at 6:00 a.m. to tell me the EPT test had turned blue! What a day that was. I had agonized that they would have to live their lives without the children they wanted so badly. I couldn't stand to even think about them being in such pain. The night Meagan was born, Kenny and I were there with Gerald and Connie in the waiting room. It was the first time I had ever done that and it was exciting. It made me regret deeply that I had not been with Karma, Mitch, and Vince when their babies were born. The look on Troy's face as he walked down the hallway toward us after it was over said everything.

Meagan Nicole Sanderson was well worth waiting for! She had blonde hair and blue eyes and we decorated their house with a sign and balloons the day they brought her home. Troy took her in the house and gave her a tour, talking to her and welcoming her home, catching it all on video. When Meagan, who was the perfect little girl, born to Karma, Mitch and Vince's perfect little brother (I am quoting Mark Lowry here... LOL), was three years old she was blessed with a baby brother who was named Tyler Roderick Sanderson. Tyler had blonde hair and blue eyes too. I stayed with Meagan the night Tyler was born and when Troy called at about 3:00 a.m. to tell me they had a boy it woke Meagan up. She was disappointed at first that he was a boy but in the next breath was telling me how she loved him. Next thing I knew we were in the living room watching Scoobie-Doo! When Tyler was two years old, Troy told me it was a good thing they had Meagan first because Tyler would have been an only child!

One day Karissa invited me to the annual Thanksgiving luncheon they have at the Methodist church. While we were enjoying our lunch, she mentioned that she would like to be back in church. (She had gone to church every Sunday before they were married) and she said Troy knew it. As my heart leaped for joy, I told her she would have to take the initiative and I was sure Troy would come with her. It wasn't long before they started coming and have been coming regularly ever since. It is such a joy to me to look almost every Sunday into the congregation and see Troy and Karissa. If Troy has to work or sleep, Karissa comes anyway. The only time neither of them are there is if the kids are sick or when they are working in the nursery. Sometimes Meagan comes to "big" church too and she enjoys it. Not only that, she listens. She is just like Troy in that she has never been a kid, always a little grownup. Tyler is more like his Uncle Vince…always busy! I am so thankful for all of my family. Life would be nothing without them and their love. They all make me feel loved and needed and that is what life is all about. Loving God and loving each other.

Kenny's son David and his wife Lisa have a beautiful little girl named Stephanie Ann. David and Lisa were engaged when Kenny and I married, and they were married about six months after we were. It was a big wedding and reception in Rockford, and we had a good time. They were living in Naperville at the time of their wedding, and both had good jobs. Then Lisa got pregnant and things started going wrong. She had a hard pregnancy that kept her in bed for months. Then she had a hard delivery and hemorrhaged afterward and that set her back some more.

We went up to visit them the weekend after Stephanie was born, to see the baby and to clean their apartment for them. It was a good thing we did. Lisa was trying to nurse the baby and couldn't get her to nurse. We tried a bottle, and she wasn't interested in that either. It wasn't long until I realized something was wrong because the baby was completely lethargic. I told them they had better take her to the hospital and they did. She was dehydrated and would have been hospitalized if they had waited until morning. As it was, they gave her Pedialyte, which she drank hungrily, and she was soon a normal, snuggly, wiggly little newborn baby.

As a result of all the lost time at work, Lisa lost her job. They would hire her in a different, lower paying position but that was not acceptable. They moved to Rockford and lived in her parent's basement for three years until they could get back on their feet. For a while David drove back and forth from Rockford to Chicago to work but he eventually found a job in Rockford. Lisa finally got a good job and they have a nice home of their own now. Stephanie is in kindergarten already and loves it. I am sure she will be a very good student. She has dark hair and very dark eyes with the longest and thickest eyelashes I have ever seen. She is a sweet little girl, and we always enjoy her when they come to visit.

The night my dad passed away, Lisa and David were here for a visit and were planning to leave the next morning. Lisa knew I was fretting because the living room carpet was dirty and there would be a lot of people in and out. She and David helped Kenny get that house cleaned up for me and I really appreciated it. She just reminded me of how we cleaned their house for them when Stephanie was born. I was able to do what I needed to do for Dad's funeral and for Mom without worrying for a moment about what was going on at home. David and Lisa extended their visit so they could attend the funeral and then left along with all of my kids and their families. They even stayed for the dinner the church had for us, which was one of the biggest ones they have done, and that made us all feel more like family than ever.

Troy. Mitch, Vince, Karme, Me

Chapter Nineteen
In The End

I know I have talked a lot about the health problems that Mom and Dad had through the years. Until you have been a caregiver, you don't think much about it. There are valuable lessons to be learned and great satisfaction in knowing that you are doing the best you can and will have no regrets. It starts gradually and you can be well into the process before you realize it.

Mom had a hysterectomy when she was in her forties. She had a nervous breakdown when she was still in her forties. She recuperated and accomplished a lot in her fifties. By the time she was sixty she was starting another nervous breakdown. She had a bad fall that ultimately resulted in shoulder replacement surgery. Then she began having serious kidney infections that would require week-long stays in the hospital. She got to the point she was sometimes having more than one of those a year. She became lethargic, lost her balance and started falling down a lot. One of the falls resulted in a badly broken ankle that required an ambulance ride to Quincy and surgery on the ankle. Every time any of these things happened, Karen and I would either stay at the hospital and sleep on couches in the waiting rooms or drive back and forth every day. Eventually, Mom ended up in Quincy on an emergency basis because she was about to die of kidney poisoning. That was one of the worst things that has happened. They managed to drain the kidney and then we were into a once-a-month checkup at Illini Hospital and three or four more times of going to Quincy to have the kidney drained. We finally decided to take her to Springfield to see a different urologist. He told us the kidney should have come out a long time ago.

If you have never given a helpless adult a bath and dressed them and driven them to the hospital before the sun comes up, you can't begin to imagine. All of this in a motel room, not at home…trying not to let the urine-soaked sheets soil the mattress on the bed. The surgery was horrendous. Mom was in intensive care for quite a while. They had her hands tied down the whole time, but she could still manage to pull out tubes and needles and everything else they had stuck in her. Six months later, we had her at Illini having emergency surgery for a bowel obstruction. This surgery was worse than the kidney surgery and was a result of damage done by the kidney surgery. The doctor told me the next day he was very pleased and surprised that Mom lived through the night. That has been two years ago. These are just the highlights of all that has happened to Mom.

Dad was more fortunate. He was never in the hospital until he had a heart attack when he was sixty-one years old. Then he was OK until he was sixty-nine. He came down with pneumonia which turned into a serious lung infection called empyema. He ended up in Springfield hospitals for nearly three months. After weeks of treatment, they finally decided he was well enough to have a thirty to seventy percent chance of surviving a drastic heart valve and aneurism surgery he had to have or die. We truly believed he would die on the operating table. He didn't. He had several setbacks and plenty of ups and downs, but the day did come when we brought him home to live another fourteen years. During this time in Springfield, Mom was so scared of losing him she was taking dozens of nerve pills a day and we literally had to hold her by both arms and help her walk wherever we needed to go. I felt like this nightmare would never be over.

I do recall one funny thing. I'm not sure there would be more than that to tell anyway! One night, Mom and I were almost asleep in our hard little beds at St. Johns North Hospital when the fire alarm went off. Mom was already in a deep drugged sleep. No matter what else she did, she always had to sleep in a silly looking pink satin sleep cap to protect her hair. Karen had gone home to Pittsfield for the night and it was all I could do to hold her up on her feet because I couldn't wake her up completely, but I grabbed that sleep cap off of her head and said, "I'm not taking you outside with that silly looking thing on your head." It actually made her chuckle. The fire was a false alarm!

Dad managed to live through all of Mom's troubles until she got really bad with the kidney problems. He had a couple of light strokes and then died of pneumonia before she had any of the kidney failures or radical surgeries. I have only told you the major things. There was lots of mundane care while they were still at home...filling pill boxes, getting prescriptions filled, paying bills, giving suppositories, changing wet or dirty beds, trying to get them to eat right, doing the Walmart shopping, cleaning Dad's urinals, arranging for Lifeline after talking them into it and listening to complaints about the help from the health department just to name a few.

I know this sounds like I am complaining or bragging about how good Karen and I have been to Mom and Dad, but I'm not. It was very difficult at times, but guess what, I had more quality time with my parents during this period in their lives than I ever had before. It gave me a chance to make up for the times I had neglected them when I was young. They weren't going anywhere and I had definitely slowed down so we had time to really get to know each other. I still have some time left with Mom and we have a lot of laughs just like we did with Dad. I wouldn't take anything for these memories, even the bad ones. We have always found strength in our faith in God, and we know we will all be together and healthy again in heaven someday.

Chapter Twenty
My Testimony for Jesus

The story of my life would not be complete or have any real meaning without my testimony of how God has worked in my life. Apart from God there is no life. My biggest regret is that it took me so many years to realize that fact and do something about it.

Most people can tell you exactly when they were saved but I really can't do that. There are differences in doctrine that I am aware of, making it difficult to know for sure exactly what happened when. I thank God that I do know I am saved and never have any doubts about it, so it really doesn't matter anyway.

When I was eleven years old, Mom took us to a revival meeting at First Baptist church here in Pittsfield. That particular evening, I happened to be worried about a test we were having at school the next day. I just knew I was going to flunk that test. As I listened to the preacher talk, I knew I needed to make the decision to accept Jesus as my Savior. I prayed and asked God to let me pass my test the next day and promised Him if he would do that, I would go forward the next night and ask Him to save me. I passed the test, and I knew I had made a promise I needed to keep. Besides, I wanted to be saved so I would know I would go to heaven when I died. It had been made clear that Jesus was the way and I accepted Him and trusted Him as best I knew how.

Mom was saved the night before and she meant business! We were in church from that day forward. It wasn't long until a Southern Baptist Church was started in Pittsfield, and we joined it along with two of my aunts and several cousins. We all grew up in Calvary Baptist Church which will be celebrating its 50th anniversary in the year 2000. Mom and Karen and I missed being charter members of the church by just a few weeks. We went to church on Sunday morning, Sunday night, and Wednesday night. Mom was also active in the ladies' mission group. Back then we had revival meeting for two weeks at a time every year if not twice a year. And there was Bible school for two weeks every summer right after school was out.

When I started high school and got interested in all that goes with being in high school, I found it a little trying to be forced to go to church first, before anywhere else. I knew it was important and didn't really fight it, I just became less interested. When I married right after high school and moved to Colorado I was surprised to discover that I missed going to church and Sunday school. It didn't take Satan long to get me used to not going and I soon found myself being glad I was on my own at last and could make my own decisions. Occasionally I would feel a little guilty, like the summer we had neighbors who got up every Sunday morning and left their apartment at about 9:00 a.m. I knew where they were going and I knew we should be doing that too. But we didn't.

After the marriage fell apart and I was back in Illinois living with my folks, I overheard a conversation between Mom and Granny Bide. I knew I didn't have the peace and joy they were talking about. I began to cry and told them something was wrong with me because I didn't have that peace and joy. I was back in church (I was living with Mom again) but I didn't really feel at home there. It had been a long time. Well, Mom and I and Granny Bide prayed together and I rededicated my life. I can't honestly say I felt all that much better after we prayed but I had done all I knew to do and trusted God to keep His promise of salvation if we ask for it. I felt at home in church after that and made my decision public by being baptized again.

Then followed the second marriage and thirteen years of regular church attendance, singing in the choir, teaching Sunday school, etc., and it was good but it was hard. By the end of that time period, I was very tired. I had a big family and I found Sunday to be the hardest day of the week. The kids never stopped giving me a hard time about going to church so of course I was tired. I had been trying to serve God without His help. We didn't talk about God's love or Jesus and His ultimate sacrifice when we were home. I didn't "teach my children in our getting up and lying down, in our going out and coming in, in the morning and in the evening." We didn't read the Bible together and pray together like we should have. The kids gave me a hard time because I was trying to teach them God was important without living like God was important. It just doesn't work that way. We need to begin praying for our kids before they are born and pray with them after they are born! They have to see that we love God all the time, not just at church.

Then came the chapter in my life I didn't want to talk about, but which turned out to be one of the most important chapters. I have already told how God never gave up on me. No matter what I did, or did not do, I never stopped feeling guilty and I never stopped loving God deep down in my heart. I knew Jesus was the answer to all my problems and the Holy Spirit never left my side. When I was finally filled with the Spirit, I became a different person. This is where the confusion comes in that I mentioned in the beginning of my testimony. I have had lengthy discussions with several pastors, Christian friends, and Spirit-filled family members. Most believe I was saved as a child, but a couple have said they think it was during the revival meeting when I asked God to fill me with His Spirit. I have to confess I don't know for sure, but I will know when I get to heaven. It doesn't matter anyway because I *know* I am saved and that is the real issue.

The thing I regret is that I wasted so many years, doing things the hard way without God's help, or not doing anything for Him at all. I was probably past forty years old before I read the Bible through for the first time. After I did that, I got the "Big Picture" of what and who God is and what His plan is for us. There is more to life than just living and dying (to quote the words of a popular Christian song). We are to love and serve God with all our heart, soul, and mind. And we are to love each other as we love ourselves. If we do this, other people will know that we belong to God and will know it is important.

You can't really know God until you study His word. This I learned when I did a study at home with a book called *A Survival Kit*. I was so excited about it I had a home study at my house a few years later and several young adults attended. It was wonderful for me and I hope it was for them. Memorizing scripture is hard work, but it pays off big time! *A Survival Kit* took three months to complete, and it whetted my appetite. When it came time for *Masterlife* I couldn't wait.

There is nothing more powerful than praying with other Christians. Praying alone is powerful, praying corporately in church is powerful, praying with family over a meal can be powerful, but earnest, heartfelt prayer with a fellow believer is indescribable. We don't do it nearly enough. We don't do enough of any kind of praying for that matter.

God created us and saved us because He wants us to talk to Him. He talks to us through the Bible and through our conscience. Sometimes He talks to us through other people. We need to be the kind of person God can talk to others through. God depends on us to be the vessel through which He does His work here on this earth.

Praise is also very powerful. It will lift your spirits when you are down, and it should flow out of us uncontrollably. It is easy for me to remember when I found it almost impossible to tell someone how much God meant in my life. Now, after twenty years of getting to know Him through worship, Bible study, prayer and praise, I look for opportunities to guide people into thinking about God. I don't believe in beating people over the head with a Bible, but I do believe in letting them know where I stand.

As you can see, if you read this whole book, I learned all of life's lessons the hard way. It takes a long time to become a mature Christian and if you do it the way I did, it will take many years. We have no knowledge of how many years we have to live on this Earth and that is the tragedy. I am so thankful to God, my Christian relatives, especially my children, and my Christian friends for their influence in my life. As I have said before, and it bears repeating over and over: There is no life apart from God!

The Bible tells us to love God from our youth. Think how much pain and suffering we would be spared if we lived our lives according to God's will from the time we are very young. That is why God wants us to give our lives over to Him when we are young. He wants not only to save our souls and give us life after death with Him, but He also wants to save our lives while we live on this Earth. He wants to give us the love, joy, peace, patience, gentleness, goodness, faith, teachableness, and self-control that are the proof that we are a child of God and truly filled with His Holy Spirit. God is so good…life in Him is so good, and once more…There is no life apart from Him.

Epilogue

Now that I am in my "golden years" it is amazing to me how good God has been, even though I didn't always appreciate it. Or even realize it for that matter. I could have written twice as much as I did in this book, talking about my Heavenly Father, my spiritual journey, my life in general, especially my kids, grandkids and my many good friends. I have merely skimmed the surface. I didn't want to put you to sleep so I tried to relate just a few of the important things, sad things and funny things.

I hope no one will feel left out or slighted in any way. I didn't talk much about Karen, the in-laws, the grandchildren, or my best friends. If I had I would never get this project finished. If each of you write your story someday, it will get done without me!

It has been a year or more since I started this project, and a lot has happened in that year. I know a lot more will happen, God willing, before this story is really finished, but I hope and pray that the worst is behind me and the best is yet to come.

I know you all know how much I love each and every one of you. I just want to say it again...I LOVE EACH AND EVERY ONE OF YOU FOREVER! My greatest hope is that we will all spend eternity together.

From the kids...

Mom was always there for me when I needed her, ALWAYS. She was a fun mom and grandma and a great storyteller. I wish I could be just like her! I cherish the times we shared the last few years. Some great fun, some not so much. Kenny, thank you for loving our mom and taking such great care of her. Love you both! Mom knew we were publishing her book and she was so excited! I just regret that she passed away before she was able to hold it in her hands, but I know that she would be very happy and proud. Never a days goes by that I don't think of her! She was a joy all the way up to the end!!

Karma

You're the greatest mom ever. I remember as a kid growing up, all my friends thought you were the best and always wanted to come to our house. I always considered you my best friend... talked to you about everything, but I think the greatest thing you gave me besides loving me is simply giving me a healthy self esteem. You helped me to believe in myself, that anything was possible, I could do anything I wanted to do and have the confidence that everything would work out fine. So I moved off into adult life with no fear, because of that. Love you Mom.

Mitch

I want to say how much I appreciate you for my entire life, you have been the one who has been there for me through all times good and bad. I appreciate that. I also want Kenny to know how much I appreciate everything he has done for me ever since he has been in our family and how much he takes care of you. I love you both.

Troy

I love you deeply. I'll never forget the way you loved us as kids and as adults. A few years ago, going through some stuff with my family, I was staying overnight at your house and was overwhelmed with sadness. I was laying on your bed crying. You came in and comforted me, told me it was going to be okay, it was okay to cry and okay to feel the way I was feeling. I'll never forget the impact of that feeling of love, acceptance, guidance and comfort—what that was like. I remember sharing with my dad and he said, too, how gifted you are at comforting people and making them feel accepted for who they are, where they're at and making them feel better. As kids, sitting on the chair, snuggling up with ya...you were always supportive and made me feel confident about myself. The way you loved me has taught me how to love myself...things that I can hand down. I hate that I don't see you as often as I should but I think about you, I love you and I know that I'm in your heart. When you tell me you've been thinking about me I believe it. Through the struggles I had changing my life from a place that I didn't want to be to the place where it is now, you've always been accepting and supportive of that too so...comfort, support, reinforcement and encouragement are your spiritual gifts. I'm grateful for you and that you're my grandmother. I love you.

Kristopher

My two fondest memories of you are sitting in the big rocking chair either on your lap or next to you while you read some of the stories out of the storybooks you have. The other one is being allowed to get a bowl of ice cream with chocolate swirls in it with a whole lot of Hershey's chocolate syrup!

Leslie

Everybody has great memories of you, I have so many! My favorites were always being perched on the side of your chair while you ate peppermints, we drank coffee and you'd make little jokes about your buffalo breath, but I really loved the smell of your breath in the morning! Isn't that funny?! And when we went to church, I would rub the cold skin on the back of your arm! Fletcher does that to me now! I think about you every time. You're a great storyteller. That is so much of what I think about you, all the stories you had to tell me. I remember when I would come stay with you in the summer, I would love to sit on the chair and listen to you talk. I wanted to listen to you tell me everything. Dad said something about how you raised him to have self-esteem and confidence and he passed that onto me which is something that I really value, something I love. It's kinda hard not to get teary when I think about you. I used to carry your autobiography around. I put stickers all over it and carried it around to tell everybody how awesome my grandma was and all of the funny stories in there. You're a dynamic woman, full of love and grace! Always so classy with your face on, drawers of make up and jewelry, and the necklace you had with the gold balls that were etched. I loved to play with that stuff. Every time Fletcher wants to be just like me and play dress up in my clothes, I think about doing that with you. I just idolized you when I was a kid! I hope you know that everybody loves you a whole lot! I love you grandma.

Cacey

Hey Connie, thank you for being a great grandma to me these past 10 years. You've accepted me as one of your own and I appreciate it. I remember once when I was at your house painting, crafting, or making peanut clusters, you know, "one glob at a time". We went out to get food and when I was in the car with you I thought to myself, "This lady's crazy!" I don't know why, but I did, ha! I love ya so much that, well…you remember "the incident"? I'm only referring to it because I know it'll make you laugh even though it's embarrassing. One night we were at your house and when it was time to leave, I got up and kissed you plain, blank on the mouth! You know I gotta love ya. But yeah, I really do love you and appreciate you, the mom that you've been to Troy and the awesome Mother-in-law you've been to my mom. You're just…really great!

Kaitlyn

Some of my favorite memories I have of you when I was growing up, I got to spend a week with you each summer and Pittsfield was my favorite place to go. Loved, loved, loved the house on Kellogg St. When I think about going to Mamaw's house in the summer that's what I think of. And I think about going with you to the bank out west when it was your turn to have a shift there, it was just you and I acting silly, of course. Playing charades…you may or may not remember that. Running coins through the sorter, typing on the typewriter, it was just a big time for a kid. And being at the store with you and watching you enjoy the overhead music and you shaking your hips a little bit, it just cracked me up and it cracked you up that it cracked me up. And of course- the one you love to tell the most- laying in bed measuring our legs to see who had the longer legs. So, those are wonderful memories for me and you have always been my fun Grandma I love so much.

Livi

Hi Grandma, it's Meagan and Toryan. I wanted to share some of my favorite memories. I always looked forward to coming over after church on Sundays to have lunch, having sleepovers in the back bedroom and coming over in the summer to watch (Pappy Drew It???) I'm so grateful for all the time I got to spend with you growing up. We love you so much.

Meagan

My favorite thing about you is that you are really funny and you always give good advice. Love you!

Kate

I love you because you let me have those mints.

Kara

My favorite memory of you is when you tried to bottle flip with us!

Luke

My favorite thing about you is your sense of humor.

Levi

I was just talking to mom about you and remembering after I had stayed with you, I'd miss you, so I would rearrange my room, my bathroom and everything else as much as possible to make it feel like I was still at your house! I always loved to, and still do, use the Oil of Beauty lotion because every time I smell that, I think of you. It made me feel like I was close to you. Also, I thought it was awesome that you would let me stay up late and watch Jay Leno. I thought that was cool because most grandmas would be like "go to bed" at 9:00 but you let me stay up late and watch it with you. Then I'd come home and watch it, I especially loved the headlines segment, because that's what you liked. I love how blunt and snarky you are and I think I get my sassy personality from you. I always thought that was one of the best things about you, that you never sugarcoat anything, you tell it like it is and you're hilarious when you do it! I love you very much.

Karissa

I love you Mamaw and Kenny. Love you all. Kenny, I love you too and I love you Mamaw.

Jase

I always remember the time you let me play Animal Jam on your computer and you told us stories about your past. Stuff that was always fun to hear and going to travel around Pittsfield was pretty fun as well, seeing where you grew up and stuff.

Caden

I have so many memories! The first one is the smell of your facial lotion, I think a lot of us have that fond memory when we smell Oil of Olay, even just looking at the bottle when shopping I think of you. Secondly, when you taught me "Oh little playmate". I love that song and I've sung it to my children, so that's special to me. You would always read to us from your storybooks. There were stories we preferred and read over and over, but I just loved just the experience of being read to. I would be remiss if I didn't mention that we loved teasing you because you would sniff three times before turning over. I loved how we giggled and giggled one night when you first moved to the little house about the sniffing before you turn over, it was ALWAYS THREE TIMES. Also, I don't think very many people know but, when I was about 11, you sat me down to talk with me about my unruly eyebrows. You sent me to the bathroom with tweezers and instructions. Thanks to you, I've had well manicured eyebrows ever since. Your nails were always perfectly painted and shaped. I always aspired to have wonderful nails, so I always have mine painted. You gave me lots of tips how to get that perfect manicure. These things may not seem significant but they truly are. But the eyebrow thing, that was an experience! I'm a seasoned pro at eyebrow shaping now! Another thing is the time we had to be with all the cousins, I mean we would just run all over the house and play in every room! The summer you had the pool was really fun. And every year we looked forward to the famous Christmas cookies. It was truly a joy to see them laid out on the counter when we arrived and then obviously, eating them because they were so delicious. I love that tradition. I think Christmas would be my favorite memory, when everyone's there. Christmas is still my favorite time, I love the memories of Christmas gatherings, the big tree and how we would all do presents and get jammies. All those things are really special. Some of these memories are funny and we laugh about them but, they are all meaningful. You have shaped our lives in big and small ways. Some of us have really great eyebrows now and some of us have really great nails. We also have great stories, songs to sing to our children and Christmas traditions to pass down too! I love you.

Kirra

I don't have memories from long ago but the memories I do have are very special to me. I love going to your house, it reminds me of being a kid and going to my grandparents house, just the feel of it. It makes me feel all warm and cozy inside. I love visiting both of you and I want to say thank you so much for making me feel welcome and accepted into the family. Love you.

Sherri

I was extremely blessed to marry into such a wonderful family with the best mother in law ever!! My favorite story about Connie is how she went to my dad and told him that they needed to set her son, Troy, up with me. My dad told her that if I found out, I wouldn't have anything to do with him, so they had to just pray. So, Connie and my dad prayed that Troy and I would get together. Now we have been married 12 years! I miss my talks with her, I miss her red hot jello and I miss listening to her boss everyone around! She really is the best mother in law and I will be forever grateful to her!

Kristi

When I first met Connie, David and I were newly engaged. Within minutes, it was as if I had known her all my life. We could sit for hours and talk, laugh and even cry. She offered advice when asked and would give the honest truth even if we weren't quite ready to hear it. During some very difficult times, she was the one person I knew would be there for us. She would offer comfort and PRAYERS!! She was the first person I ever knew that was the epitome of the title of prayer warrior. I so looked forward to her coming to our house for visits and I was always so excited to go to Pittsfield and visit her and Kenny. David and I were so grateful to have her as a bonus Grandma for our kids. She was the person to tell me that our 4 day old daughter wasn't quite acting right. Within a few hours we had her at the immediate care and Connie was right! Stephanie was dehydrated after being home for less than 24 hours from the hospital. Because of Connie and my best friend Ann, we were allowed to come home that night instead of being admitted to the hospital. Ann and Connie took turns giving Stephanie Pedialyte every 2 hours for 14 hours. I can't even imagine what would have happened had Connie not been there. And oh the back rubs she was famous for giving to her grandbabies. It would calm them in a way that I was never able to replicate. We feel so blessed to have had Connie in our lives. We love her so very much and miss her dearly.

Lisa

My favorite memory was being able to take her on trips to places she had never been. I'm so glad that Karma was able to have time to help Kenny care for her in her last days.

Karl

www.ingramcontent.com/pod-product-compliance
Lightning Source LLC
Chambersburg PA
CBHW071413070526
44578CB00003B/569